BURT!
THE UNAUTHORIZED
BIOGRAPHY

BURT!
THE UNAUTHORIZED BIOGRAPHY

BY MARC ELIOT

A JOAN HITZIG McDONELL BOOK

Published by
Dell Publishing Co., Inc.
1 Dag Hammarskjold Plaza
New York, New York 10017

ISBN: 0-440-00876-X

Printed in the United States of America

First printing—July 1982

for J.
... *And the starting five*

I'm one of the most beloved grass roots heroes in America, and if you don't come out here and start lovin' me I'm gonna kick your ass.

Burt Reynolds as "The Bandit,"
SMOKEY AND THE BANDIT, PART II

BURT!
THE UNAUTHORIZED
BIOGRAPHY

one

Buddy Reynolds was only fifteen years old, but he'd had enough. Things hadn't really been right ever since Burt Reynolds, Sr. had moved the whole family out of Waycross, Georgia south to fancy Riviera Beach, Florida, that summer of 1954. Waycross, a smudgy little boondock squeezed behind poverty and across the street from misery, U.S.A., was all right with Buddy; everyone there had the same amount of nothing. "Rivera," as Buddy called it, was something else, a bankbook of a town on Florida's elite gold coast, a martini away from silky West Palm Beach where Burt, Sr. had been offered a job with the police force. With a wife and three children to tend, work was where you found it; acceptance, that was something you earned along the way.

The rest of the family may have been impressed with this acceptance business, but not Buddy. He wasn't even allowed to use his own name—Burt Reynolds, Jr. He was "Buddy"; a seedling, a spruce, a little acorn, that would do—good enough for now. The unspoken rule in the South between father and son was simple—"You

ain't a man until your father tell you you're a
man." Affection? Buddy and Burt could hardly
look at each other: talking mostly in grunts and
groans colliding with yessirs and no sirs. Pride?
Hell, boy, you better toe the line. As Burt would
recall years later, "Going to hug my father was
like trying to hug a statue of Lincoln. You just
didn't." No sir. Getting too close could get you
whomped. Now whomping, that was one thing;
being able to take it, that was another. It was all
part of growing up southern, and part Cherokee
Indian on top of that.

Burt Reynolds, Sr. could tell you a lot about
acceptance. He'd spent a lifetime earning it.
Now, he was police chief of West Palm Beach.
His assignments might be anything from rescu-
ing a cat up a tree to tackling a crazy killer. No
sweat, no complaints. The gold coast of Florida
was a far cry from the Cherokee reservation
where he'd been born and raised. Burton Reynolds grew up fast and tough. Fern, the young,
pretty woman he chose to make Mrs. Reynolds,
was a sweet Italian girl whose strong dark features weren't that markedly different from his
own. Together they settled in as Burton determined to make it in the white man's world. Law
and order, respect for the land, pride in the
family, reverence for the head of the house,
earning the honest dollar—these were the rules
that led toward acceptance, a social reward so
coveted to those born without.

An accepted man's greatest offering to his
community were his children, his continuation.
So if either of the two young Reynolds' boys, or

even the little girl, Nancy Ann, stepped out of line they'd get their hides tanned, but good.

If Buddy had to take it from the chief, he sure as hell wasn't going to take it from anybody else. Not his older brother, Jim, bigger and tougher than Buddy, and always a little too ready to punch the kid out; not the prissy white shoe'd boys at school who made fun of him, who called him "Greaseball" and "Mullet," referring to the gang Buddy had fallen in with, the young toughs with cigarettes behind their ears and duck tails behind their necks who hung out down by the Everglades; fishing turf, muscle tone mentality. It didn't take Buddy long to realize there was one sure way of protecting yourself in a tough crowd—join a tougher one.

If being in a gang gave Buddy the type of pride that comes with hitching up your pants by your wrists and sticking your jaw out, it filled Burt, Sr. with disgust. Chief Reynolds was fast becoming a legend of law and order in the jails and bars of southern Florida, someone who played by the book. The story they loved to tell most was the one when Chief Reynolds collared this guy who then offered him, on the spot, a paper bag filled with fifteen thousand dollars in cash, "to look the other way." Chief Reynolds made this sucker eat the paper bag. He was tough, and not impressed with young Buddy and his cheap gang dramatics. So it didn't really surprise anyone when Buddy didn't show up for dinner one night. He'd had it, that's all, he'd packed it in and run away. He was sure Burt Sr. wouldn't even notice he was gone.

*   *   *

Buddy wasn't going anywhere in particular, just running away. He was fifteen, small for his age, afraid of nothing. He'd taken it from the biggest and the toughest; he could go on taking it forever if he had to. Forever lasted one week, as far north as South Carolina where he was picked up by the police Chevy red-light, four-barrel 409. The charge: vagrancy. At the station Buddy told them his name and that his father was the police chief of West Palm Beach, Florida. It didn't surprise Buddy when the Carolina cops told him they were going to lock him up anyway. They'd called his old man who told them he thought a few days behind bars might teach the boy a lesson. They gave him a week in the slammer to think it over, with recreation time as a water boy on a chain gang.

Buddy returned to "Rivera" but not to the chief's house. He'd had enough police for awhile. Instead, he moved in with one of the tough short-haired girls from his street gang. Occasionally, Buddy would run into his father on the streets of West Palm Beach. They'd stare at each other for a long time. "How are you boy?" Burt, Sr. would finally ask in his formal, controlled tone. Buddy, already in the habit of turning his head and talking it seemed to no one in particular, a mannerism that would one day drive women crazy in wide screen and technicolor, might grunt something back before shuffling on. He couldn't understand why the chief wouldn't put his hand out to make peace, never figuring on making the first move himself. After a year Buddy came back home to live, but the distance between the chief and his young warrior remained wide.

Buddy was a junior now at West Palm Beach High School. The chip on his shoulder might have grown into a full-scale lumber yard if two things hadn't happened: if he hadn't met Ann Lawler, a pretty co-ed he thought for sure he was going to marry, and if he hadn't decided to race Vernon Rollison, the fastest kid in school. He didn't punch out Vernon's face because Ann convinced him it wasn't the "right" thing to do, that he could embarrass the uppity Vernon by outclassing him, and he could outclass him by outrunning him. Ann Lawler was the first of a long list of women who would represent the type Buddy figured he "should" be with—clean, intelligent, willing and able to take care of him, extremely popular in the right circle. For the rest of his school career and later on through the halcyon days of New York and Hollywood Burt would fluctuate between "Ann's," quality women he thought he should be seen with, and the good-time girls he really dug. Today, Burt credits Ann Lawler with being the first to give him confidence. Yet while they were both going to West Palm Beach, Buddy had to pick her up for dates by ringing the bell at the servant's entrance to her parents' estate.

As for Vernon, no one really remembers how the race came about. It may have been over sodas in the school lunchroom, or on the field after classes. Buddy, always ready to swing a hard left

at the first sign of trouble, gritted his teeth for
Ann and accepted a challenge to find out who
was really the fastest kid in school. Buddy was
shocked when five hundred students turned out
to watch the race. He slipped out of his moccasins and ran barefoot, literally leaving Vern behind in a cloud of track dust. As Burt told an
interviewer years later, "One day I was a mullet,
the next day I was Buddy. In the back of my
mind I thought, boy, if there ever comes a time
when you can't outrun anybody, you'll go back
to being a mullet . . . and sometimes you
don't run faster, you run over."

If Burt had been thinking about maybe dropping out of school and getting a job as a
mechanic or something, things were now very
different. Almost immediately, the coach of the
football team asked Buddy if he'd be interested
in trying for a spot as a running back. A couple
of touchdowns later, Buddy was one of the Saturday heroes of West Palm Beach High. He was
in demand not only on the football field, but also
on the baseball diamond, the track oval, and the
basketball court. His low grades, which reflected
his anger and defiance at authority—be it father
or teacher—began to improve. By his senior year
he was one of the most popular kids in school.
Instead of being the closeout to his academic
career it had become the first step. He was courted by many of the biggest football colleges in
the country. He'd turned the trick all right. He
was now a jock. It seemed there was nothing
that could stop him now.

two

Notre Dame was sure it had Buddy Reynolds set to play for its backfield. Few high school stars turned down a chance to play for the Grand Lady, on a full scholarship. If you were good enough for Notre Dame, you were good enough for the pros. For Saturday's heroes, the rest of the week could be pretty soft; lots of girls, cars and grades, all fast and easy.

Buddy, though, was wavering, even as he basked in the glow of being the star of West Palm Beach High. Sure enough, he declined Notre Dame's offer. Maybe he was too intimidated by the fear of having to prove himself all over again. For whatever reason, he signed a letter of intent to play for the University of Miami. All in all, twenty-six universities offered Buddy full-time free passes. Just as it seemed certain he would be attending Miami, he switched and decided he'd go to Florida State University, a second-rate football school at best with absolutely no gridiron tradition; and for a very good reason. As football coach Tom Nugent craftily pointed out to young Buddy, Florida State had been an all-girls school until 1948.

17

The ratio of girls to guys in 1954, Buddy's freshman year, would be a good ten to one. The fact that the school was second-rate athletically didn't bother Buddy. A 5'11" runner weighing a chunky 175 could get torn up pretty fast messing with the really big boys. Being a stand-out in a mediocre crowd was like, well, like star-ring in a "B" movie and getting rave reviews.

As a freshman at Florida State, Buddy was re-quired to room with a senior in order to get ac-quainted with the rules and regulations of the college. Buddy shared a dorm with Ronny King, the biggest guy on the football team and a ladies man in his own right. Buddy was quiet at first, careful to keep his side of the dorm room neat, lining up his moccasins in a row at the side of his bed, hanging his clothes precisely, keeping his books in order on his desk. The first sign they were going to be pals came when they discovered they shared the same nightmare. It became a daily ritual. Every morning at eight o'clock, Buddy and Ronny would stare into the full-length mirror, close-up, pulling their hair up, back, down around the sides and up again. They were both losing hair faster than FSU's football team was losing games! Ronny would shrug, try-ing to be as philosophical as a southern college jock can be, but Burt was twisted with fear and anger that he was going to be a young, bald, former ladies' man. Maybe to prove that he still had it, he aimed his sights at the best looking freshman co-ed on campus, the much desired and as yet unattainable by any and all Jean Haden, a girl Ronny King remembers as a "blonde, sorority type, and about the nicest, toughest thing on campus." Jean was definitely the correct type, and about time too. Buddy had been pretty busy since breaking up with Ann Lawler, just after high school graduation. First there was the balle-rina-to-be, then assorted secretaries and other bouffant nine-to-fivers. When Buddy first saw Jean, though, he was determined to land her as his steady. At first he hung around Pi Psi, Jean's sorority house, waiting for a chance to meet her, marriage fantasies playing off inside his head. He had to have her, he had to, and he got her. Jean became his main girl, officially touted, officially shown off; the prime lady. They were together all the time Buddy was at Florida State. Even after they broke up, Buddy still felt deeply for her. When she married a wealthy rancher years later, Buddy couldn't put it to rest until he visited Jean and her husband on their ranch. One friend of Buddy recalls that he finally resolved his being hung up on Jean only after he met her husband and realized how happily married she really was.

He didn't do badly on the field, either, but he wasn't great. As a freshman, he did get to play in a number of games, but his playing wasn't al-ways limited to four quarters. Often, things would get out of hand at the local bar in Talla-hassee after a Saturday game. A couple of drinks with the boys and the old fight would come right back to him. There was the time in one of the jock beer joints when the other team happened to come in to down a few. Words were ex-

changed and then punches, Buddy getting in his
licks before signaling for the rest of the guys to
split to the tune of approaching police sirens. Or
the time Buddy got into a fight on the second
floor of a building and was punched clear
through the window onto the street below. It
wasn't all bloody and violent, though; there
were plenty of easy evenings spent with his fellow brothers of Phi Delta Theta in the company
of the sweet and pretty Pi Phis, parties that
would last all night, all day, and into the next
night and day.

Invariably, Buddy would take control early
on, getting requests to do the thing they all loved
to see him do—impersonate Marlon Brando in "A
Streetcar Named Desire." As one fellow student
recalls, "Buddy was real good imitating Brando.
He looked so much like him, with the high forehead. That's all he ever did. Almost everything
you'd say to him he'd give you a Brando answer
back."

Imitating Brando and playing football. He did
a fantastic Stanley Kowalski, but his football
was less than terrific. In all fairness, it wasn't entirely his fault. As a freshman, getting any playing time, even at FSU, was something of an
accomplishment. And he was small. But he was
also fast.

Perhaps his finest freshman moment came
during the FSU-Auburn game, on Auburn's field.
Buddy, #22, had the ball coming from scrim-
mage downfield, flying fifty-four yards heading
for a lightning touchdown. The Florida Seminoles
were only a second away from taking the lead

until the Auburn War Eagles, led by Fob James, caught Buddy and creamed him on the one yard line. James, who would one day be George Wallace's successor as Governor of Alabama, put the game, and Buddy, on ice, knocking the speedy left halfback out cold. This injury and a minor knee problem got Buddy the reputation of being injury-prone, a label that stuck even though he did make freshman All-Florida and All-Southern running back honors.

The Seminoles were good enough to make the Sun Bowl. While Buddy was bursting with pigskin pride, Ronny King wasn't all that thrilled. He'd much rather have spent the extra week needed for practice back home in Daytona Beach horsing around. Coach Nugent, trying to juice the team, devised a new plan, a special "I"-formation offense starring his tough backfield of Buddy Reynolds, Junior Metz, Ted Rodriquez, and King. The idea was to split the offense off either side of the quarterback to confuse and dissipate the defense of the feared Texas Western team. Buddy, Ronny and the rest of the team practiced relentlessly, chomping at the bit for the chance to dazzle Texas and Florida with their new game. Unfortunately, they never got the chance to split the "I" and work their backfield magic. They were pulverized on the field. Buddy's last game of that first season filled the locker room afterwards with soft vows of "Wait until next year" instead of boisterous shouts of "Hail, hail the gang's all here."

Although Buddy didn't have a car when he came to Florida State, being too poor to be able

to buy one, by the summer he managed to scrape
enough bread together to get his hands on a big,
fat, used Buick Eight. He loved all cars and
gunned around Tallahassee and West Palm
Beach day and night, opening the dual quads as
he roared down the flat Florida highways. Maybe
because his father was such a strict enforcer of
the law, or maybe because he was simply turned
on by speed—on the gridiron or behind the
mother of pearl steering wheel—but whatever the
reason Buddy soon got his quota of speeding
tickets. "Slow down, boy," was the litany from
the highway patrolmen he heard nearly as often
as Hank Williams' crooning coming out of the
Delco in the dash.

Buddy and Burt, Sr. still weren't getting
along. The tension at home was relieved somewhat for Mrs. Reynolds because Buddy started
to bring around some of his college pals to the
house the family was now living in up in North
Palm Beach. As Mrs. Reynolds recalled in an interview years later, even though Buddy was eas-
ing up a bit, he and the chief still had their
tempers. She described Buddy then as "A fine
boy, but he'd take so much, then blow up. He'd
get too big for his britches and his daddy would
have to straighten him out. But that's all it took.
A little straightenin' and Buddy was a good boy
again. The front steps on Friday nights used to
sound like a herd of cattle was going to charge
through the house. Buddy was always bringing
his college buddies home for the weekend, and
what times those were—with all the football
players to feed. I love it. . . ."

Apparently Buddy loved it too. College was a turn-on for him and couldn't wait to get back to campus that fall. Being a sophomore with the best looking co-ed on his arm and the toughest battle scars on his reputation made #22 the hotshot of FSU, fall '54. His growing gridiron legend stretched farther than the stands of the Tallahassee stadium. The pro scouts had heard about this speedy half-breed letterman and were drifting down to check him out. Early in the second year of his FSU career, Buddy was offered an option contract by the Baltimore Colts. (In the fifties, it was legal for pro teams to sign what amounted to "first refusal" deals with college players.) Buddy, needless to say, was on top of the world. He'd made it. To play for the legendary Colts was to play for one of the greatest pro teams of all time. Nothing could stop him now. Nothing. Acceptance, yeah!

He could hardly keep the Buick on the ground. He just loved to floor her for all she was worth. On the open road he hated more than anything being boxed in behind a "creeper," turtling along at fifty-five, maybe sixty. Which is pretty much how it was the night before Christmas, '54 when Buddy was rocketing along, blissfully oblivious, until it was too late, of the trooper coming up strong in the rearview mirror. The trooper pulled him over and gave him a ticket for speeding, citing 95 as Buddy's speed. Another ticket! His father was going to kill him. Buddy held the ticket in one hand and started down the interstate again, cutting his speed to a

benign thirty-five miles an hour and determined
to stay down there. All he needed was yet another ticket and he'd be hauled into the local
precinct for sure. However, as soon as he was
convinced the trooper was not on his tail, he bar-
reled right back up to ninety-five, making the
Buick's pretty engine purr. It would be, after all,
Christmas in a few minutes.

Out of nowhere, it seemed, the flatbed truck
appeared in front of him. A "creeper"! Too late,
Buddy stomped the power brakes; the Buick
screeching rubber as Buddy tried to hold the
wide power brake pedal flat to the floor. The
tighter he gripped the steering wheel, though, the
faster the truck's big rear end seemed to be coming up on him. And Buddy's Buick was still doing better than fifty! He realized he wasn't going
to be able to stop, that he was going to slam into
the rear end of the flatbed! About a second before death, Buddy dove for all he was worth under the dashboard of the mercifully roomy
Buick. If not for the fact that his reflexes were
pin-sharp from football practice and his body
was in peak physical condition, he probably
would have been killed instantly. The flatbed
cleanly sliced off the top half of the Buick as ef-
fortlessly as a hot knife through a stick of butter.
A second more and Buddy's head would have
rolled down the highway like a ghoulish basketball.

As it was, Buddy was pinned under the dash.
The truck driver ran to the car immediately, to
see just how bad things were. "Is anybody in
there . . . anybody alive?" the driver called

out. From within the crunch of twisted, fierce metal, Buddy screamed out for help. "I'm hurt . . . I can't move . . . call my father, he's the chief of police. . . ." The driver froze. High-tailing back to the front cabin of his truck he shifted into gear and slowly pulled the flatbed off the wreck, taking off into the night. Unfortunately, Buddy had said the ultimate wrong thing, scaring off the driver who, along with his two companions happened to be carrying a load of stolen cement blocks.

Twenty agonizing minutes passed before the police car arrived, and it almost passed by without stopping! It was dark, the road was ill-lit, it was Christmas eve, Buddy's Buick could have been a convertible pulled over. When the trooper finally realized there was something wrong, he threw his patrol car into reverse, took a good look and called for an ambulance.

Buddy still wasn't safe. It took seven hours to cut him out of the pathetic heap. By all medical accounts, in spite of Buddy's superb physical condition, it was a miracle indeed the boy survived. His spleen was crushed, a condition usually followed by hemorrhaging, then death. However, by diving beneath the dash he'd been forced into a tight fetal ball by the impact of the crash. The blood, not being able to dissipate internally or out of his body, coagulated, preventing bleed-out, shock, and death. Buddy was rushed to the nearest hospital for seven hours of emergency surgery. Besides the damage to his spleen, there were two other major injuries. His

left knee and his right knee. One was patchable.
The other was more powder than kneecap.

Buddy was on the critical list for weeks. Three
doctors worked on him full-time, hoping to prevent the young athlete from walking with a per-
manent limp. When he was finally released from
the hospital, it was obvious to everyone except
Buddy that his football days were over. The
team and Coach Nugent were slap-on-the-back
happy to see ol' Buddy up and around; they
tossed footballs on the field, cracked jokes, and
talked about the new season. Slowly, though, reality began to set in for Buddy. That vague ma-
licious anger he'd buried when he'd discovered
running was coming back; the dread he'd carried
around like an extra internal injury was starting
to ache once more—*if there ever comes a time
when you can't outrun anybody, you'll go back
to being a mullet. . . .*
There was insurance money from the accident
and a lot of time to kill while his knees healed.
Buddy didn't feel like sitting up in the stands
watching practice for a couple of months. He
took a job working for the notorious playboy,
Porfirio Rubirosa, on his Florida horse ranch, but
quickly became bored with his boots knee-deep
in horse hay. Maybe he should take a trip, go
away, let a little steam off. He picked the place
where all the rebellious lemmings fled to in those
days; that place up north where Brando, the real
Brando that is, lived and played.

*   *   *

Greenwich Village, U.S.A., the fifties; the pulse of the beatnik universe. Being an outcast was in. Young men from all over the country came to play out their fantasies in the mythic night alleys of the rebel stomping grounds, and usually without any causes. What had begun as a coffeehouse neighborhood was suddenly the new center of creative America.

Greenwich Village was slouching to the beat of a different bongo, laying down rhythms tough leather-clad kids like Buddy could get hip to. No wonder he wanted to head for New York. With his brooding good looks and his delinquent hostility, he figured to score quick and fast in Brandoville. It's not that he wanted to be an actor; he wanted to be Marlon Brando. New York was Buddy's season-long half time, an extended R and R convalescence to be filled with romance, waterfronts and women. In reality, it was a season of dishwashing at Schrafft's, depressing cold water flats, and dead-end adventures; adding up to nothing more than fuel for Buddy's determination to return to his days of football glory. By the fall he figured he was strong enough to go back.

To FSU's credit, they let him come back on scholarship to try out for the team. It was no use, though. It was painfully obvious Buddy had lost a step; the once flashy burst of speed was only last year's memory now. As one friend recalled in an interview years later, "Buddy had this style of running before he got himself banged up. He was something else again! Weaving and cutting back and forth . . . just beautiful to watch." He felt humiliated when he couldn't make the team. When he gave up his scholarship for good and left FSU, his father barked he was a quitter, not man enough to be one of the team.

A friend gave Buddy a final piece of advice. "Go back to New York. Forget football. It's all over for you."

three

"SEVENTEEN Marlon Brandos and thirteen Jimmy Deans" is the way Burt Reynolds remembers Lee Strasburg's Actor's Studio, where he began taking classes. This Brando thing he had going for him might have been hot stuff in Tallahassee, but in Greenwich Village torn tee shirts were a dime a dozen. Every actor with a high forehead seemed to squint and mumble with his head tilted and his palms face up. And Buddy had no idea what these acting teachers were talking about. Never a big reader, he felt like a cretin in class, avoiding the other students who hung out in smoky, boozy bars discussing the new poets, the Russian Revolution, or the latest play happening downtown. It didn't take long for Buddy to start shoving guys around out of frustration and insecurity. He fought with students, or drunks in late night beer joints, even panhandlers. He'd pull cab drivers out of their taxis for a bad word, no big deal he recalled years later, because "cab drivers aren't tough and aren't usually in shape, and I was. I would fight anybody at the drop of a hat, mainly because I didn't know that I could lose."

*   *   *

It was late one afternoon, or early one evening, who knew or cared. It was one of those
cheap sawdust-on-the floor bars. Buddy had already begun to tie one on. There was nothing else
to do really, the rain outside coming down the
way it can only in New York—filthy mad. Next
to Buddy sat a man with boulder shoulders,
hunched over and mean. Obscenities flew out of
his mouth offending Buddy's courtly southern
sensibilities. Cursing among the guys was all
right, but definitely not cool in front of women.
"Hey, there's a woman in here," Buddy said,
loud and firm. The other fellow turned and gave
Buddy the quick once-over. "Hey, asshole," he
mumbled as he lunged forward. Buddy locked
his foot onto the bar rail and let a sledgehammer
right sink into the guy's skull. Nobody missed
the brisk sound of crunching bone as the guy
went into orbit flying literally fifteen feet into
the air. Buddy watched in horror as he saw that
the guy had no legs. No legs! Now he lay on the
floor like an upended turtle. Not knowing what
to do, Buddy quietly apologized as he left, noticing for the first time the neatly folded wheel-
chair at the end of the bar.

Yeah, New York was turning into a real bum-
mer. There was nothing to do besides drink, eat,
read *Catcher In The Rye* for the umpteenth
time, and, on the odd day, play a little pick-up
basketball on concrete street courts, or up at the
"Y" with one of the few actors he'd met he
could get along with, a young, swaggering then-
unknown Rip Torn. When they played one-on-

one, Buddy noticed something about Torn, the way the guy drove to the basket, playing every point as if it were a game winner. It was precisely the kind of drive that Buddy had playing football; a focus for the energy, the anger, the rage. If he could only get into this acting thing the way he'd been able to play football. The first step, he knew, was to try to control his temper, to take a deep breath and try, always try to look the other way if at all possible.

Which is one of the reasons he didn't smack the next guy who asked for it, coming up to him in a bar, asking Buddy if he knew how to read. Conrad Hopkins was the fellow's name, and of course he'd meant as an actor; could he interpret? Today, Reynolds still credits Hopkins as one of the first people responsible for getting Buddy interested in serious reading. Hopkins, who frequented the actor bars, was attracted to Buddy's strength, and saw early on the possibilities of what a controlled, directed, educated Buddy Reynolds could accomplish. Almost from the day they met, Buddy began taking himself seriously as a student of the arts for the first time in his life. By the fall of 1957, Buddy Reynolds was ready to return to school one more time. At the age of twenty-one, he enrolled at Palm Beach Junior College.

In some ways it was a humbling step down from the glory of the first string football team at FSU. In other ways, it was a smart, calculated attempt to avoid further embarrassment, as well as the constant exposure to what he could never

have: the gridiron run to daylight at which he'd
once been so good. Palm Beach Junior College
was one of those two-year schools that began
springing up in the fifties across America. For
the most part, they were community supported,
meaning local taxes footed most of the tuition
bills. Since two years is not enough time to develop top athletes, the big men on campus at
junior colleges were usually the dramatics
students, on their way to associate degrees in
pre-law, pre-med, pre-teaching; or sociology if
their parents could afford to pay tuition for two
more years.

Buddy started hanging out with the drama
club, a group of outgoing, funny kids who com-
mandeered one end of the cafeteria. It was easy
for him to fit in. First, there was his Brando, to
which he had now added a dynamite Gabby
Hayes impersonation between lots of funky stories about his actually having "been there" in
Greenwich Village. Buddy's bravado was picked
up on by Watson B. Duncan III, the chairman
of the drama department. He decided to take
young Buddy under his wing, to gently guide
him through the great works of literature, waiting to be read. Buddy especially loved the classic
poets. His new hero became Lord Byron, a sort
of idealized Brando; part lady-killer, part aes-
thete; a fellow speed-demon of the spirit.

When it came time for Professor Duncan to
cast his spring production of OUTWARD
BOUND, there was little doubt as to who would
play the lead. The part was originally made famous on Broadway by John Garfield, the actor

Brando had mimicked so well in ON THE WATERFRONT. Even though, as Reynolds was to recall years later, he hardly read two lines for his audition, he got the part. Out of his performance, which was his very first appearance on a stage, he won a scholarship to study at Hyde Park Playhouse, which happened to be located in upstate New York. There was a difference this time, though. He would actually have something to do with his time besides drinking and fighting. He might even get a chance to act.

Also appearing at the playhouse that year was an actress whose star had just begun to rise. Joanne Woodward couldn't help being taken with Buddy. Although she never actually saw him perform, she was charmed by his demeanor, moved by how shy the handsome young actor was. He always carried his paper bag with lunch to the playhouse, going off to eat by himself instead of hanging around and schmoozing with the other actors. He was different, Woodward felt, special. She decided to help him out by introducing him to her agent at MCA, one of the larger talent agencies. They interviewed him and offered to represent him. Buddy was elated. He made up his mind to return to Greenwich Village rather than Palm Beach Junior College. This time, he would make a serious attempt to learn how to act. Most important, someone believed in him again. He'd been accepted. Now, all he had to do was earn it.

four

AFTER finding a place to live, a cold-water flat he shared with a couple of other actors, Buddy auditioned and was accepted for study at Sanford Meisner's Neighborhood Playhouse. The Playhouse, like the Actor's Studio, was an intense, melodramatic jangle of technique. Whyn Handman, Buddy's teacher, introduced "truth," "moment-to-moment," "improvisation," and "how to listen" to Buddy and his classmates, much to Buddy's bewilderment. The more Buddy tried to "act," the more the other students would snicker, covering their mouths to hide their chuckles. "Don't try so hard," Handman would advise Buddy, but it didn't help. All this training was supposed to open him up as an actor. Instead, it was making him more uptight than ever. Much of his work at the playhouse resembled a parody of Brando, his one-time idol fast becoming his nemesis. MCA sent him up for parts in films being cast in New York, and he was always rejected for the same reason. He looked too much like Brando. Buddy just missed out on a part in *Sayonara* because

Josh Logan decided at the last minute that having one Brando in the film was enough.

In order to support himself while he looked for acting work, Buddy did a stint in the post office and worked after-hours as a bouncer at New York's famed Roseland dance hall. In later years, Reynolds would credit his nights as a bouncer among the most valuable "training" he received.

It was because he was so physical that he finally did get his first paid acting job. One of the more obscure live TV shows coming out of New York in the fifties was something called FRONTIERS OF FAITH. One script they were doing called for a man to be hurled through a window to his death. The producers heard about this young, very physical actor and offered Buddy the job. He was elated. Let his fellow acting students work up a sweat over Chekhov! He was going to earn $132 for flying through a pane of harmless sugar glass, and on live TV!

Still in its infancy, television had no history and no experts, only gamblers. If you were game enough to try, you became the man, and Buddy Reynolds quickly became the stunt man of choice, afraid of nothing, unusually graceful for a man of his size (he'd put on twenty-five pounds since his football days, tipping the scale at 200 solid pounds). For the next two years, Buddy went through hundreds of windows, down countless stairs, over bar tops, under speeding cars, whatever. While becoming an expert stuntman, he never actually played real parts or acted a single line of dialogue. Finally, after pressing one of the producers he'd worked many times for, he got his first real try at dialogue. Gradually, his assignments became roles, and he began to speak more and stunt less. But not much less.

MCA continued to send up Buddy for roles in Broadway shows and movies, while Buddy continued to shop for an acting class where he might learn something. He took lessons with Stella Adler and Curt Conway, two more "cult" teachers of the New York style of method acting. No matter where he studied, or what he auditioned for, his Brando likeness continued to plague him. One night, while Buddy and his friends were having dinner in a New York restaurant someone pointed out that Marlon Brando was also there. Someone who knew both actors brought Buddy over to Brando's table, to make the formal introduction. Brando was less than thrilled, yawning in Buddy's face, rolling his eyes up in bored exasperation. Buddy was terrified and furious at the same time. So much so that several weeks later, on a date, after having had a couple of drinks too many Buddy declared he was going over to where Brando lived to "have it out" with him. Buddy sat on Brando's stoop for hours, giving up on the showdown when he sobered up and realized Brando wasn't going to show.

It was about this time in his career that he decided to drop "Buddy," the name he'd used since childhood. Perhaps it was on the advice of his agents that "Buddy" was too soft a name for a rugged leading-man type. Or maybe it was the fact that a friend told him what Marlon

Brando's real name was—Buddy Brando! Whatever the reason, when MCA sent him up to audition for a part in the upcoming Broadway
revival of MR. ROBERTS, it was Burt Reynolds who showed up for the audition.

He landed the role of Reber, one of the sailors
aboard ship in a City Center revival of the successful Broadway play, now tailored as a vehicle
for the very hot Charlton Heston. Heston's portrayal of Moses in THE TEN COMMAND-
MENTS the previous year assured the revival a
sell-out run, especially since the movie was still
playing to capacity crowds down the block at
the Rivoli. At the first rehearsal for the play,
Burt found himself face to face with Heston, the
first superstar he'd ever met. Stepping forward
to shake Moses' hand, Burt tripped and fell flat
on his face.

Burt's performance in MR. ROBERTS was all
right, but his agents were convinced he'd never
cut it as a legitimate New York stage actor.
They set out to convince him he'd be better off
utilizing his natural physical grace and handsome
features in television, particulary the type of action TV series Hollywood was beginning to
churn out.

In 1959, MCA arranged for Burt to audition
for Lee Marvin's "M Squad," a tough, action-
oriented cop show produced by the gravel-voiced
Marvin. Burt didn't trip over himself when he
met Marvin, but there was a stumbling block of
another sort. Marvin wanted to see some footage
of Burt, something that would show what he

looked like on camera. Since Burt had done all
of his TV work live, there wasn't a single foot of
film available on him. What he did next suggests
the type of good-natured humor Burt would display with greater frequency the more successful
he became later on. He called his mother in
Palm Beach to ask if she kept any of the eight-
millimeter baby films she'd taken of him. When
she told him she did, he asked her to send them
to him immediately. He then called Marvin to
tell him he'd found some film of himself after
all. The rest of the entourage in the screening
room didn't think Burt's joke was so funny, but
Marvin thought it was hysterical, ordering Burt
cast then and there for a featured role in an upcoming "M Squad" episode.

five

ONCE in Hollywood, Burt came under the personal guidance of Lew Wasserman of MCA, fast becoming one of the largest talent agencies in the world. Wasserman arranged for Burt to audition for a couple of hotshot west-coast MCA agents looking for fresh talent. Burt prepared two overly dramatic monologues he'd learned in acting classes back east. He was naturally a little apprehensive when he walked in to meet the agents. He started the first piece, barely getting into it when the phone rang. Before one of the agents could answer it, before he even had time to tell Burt to hold up, Burt grabbed the phone and ripped it out of the wall, furious at the interruption. After that, he figured there was no point finishing his audition and left.

The next day he got a call from one of the agents inviting him back, to talk things over. He confessed that Burt's tantrum had been the most exciting thing that had happened around the agency in weeks. Soon, Burt was popping up in all types of TV shows playing angry, physical young men. He had a featured part in "The Lawless Years," one of the new crop of TV

westerns that caught the eye of the producers of
another new series, "Laramie." Burt was asked
to audition for the title role. He didn't get the
part, but he did get something else—Wasserman's promise that Burt would soon have his own
series. MCA was, in fact, the parent company of
Universal Studios. Along with Warner Brothers,
its chief rival, Universal had become the busiest
television back lot in Hollywood. Wasserman
confirmed his commitment to Burt by offering him a seven-year contract with Universal
Studios. Don't worry, Wasserman assured Burt
after "Laramie" fell through. Something would
happen soon enough.

Within weeks Burt was put up for, and got the
role of Ben Frazer, pilot of the Enterprise, the
sternwheeler of the new, hour-long "Riverboat"
series. Even though the director and many of the
producers objected to Burt's casting—some quite
vehemently—the part was his, and he determined
to make the most of it. "Riverboat" was Universal's answer to rival Warner Brothers' smash
ABC series, "Maverick." "Riverboat," on NBC,
began broadcasting in September, 1959. It
starred Darren McGavin as Grey Holden, a
"fun-loving romantic, expert fist-fighter, rum-
runner, swordsman, dock foreman, and soldier of
fortune" as the press release for the show explained. His copilot on the Enterprise was Ben
Frazer, orphaned river-rat side-kick, played by
Burt.

Things went wrong the very first day. Burt
and McGavin weren't able to hit it off; McGavin
ordering everyone around, telling people what to

do as if he were the captain of the show as well as the boat. Burt sized up McGavin. "I will say this about him," Burt was quoted later, "he's going to be a very disappointed man on the first Easter after his death." McGavin's resentment of Burt was easy to explain, the youngster was just too good. Burt projected a dark, brooding strength, while the slick McGavin seemed out of place in the muddy waters of the Mississippi. McGavin, though, was coming off the hit series, "Mike Hammer," and still carried a lot of weight with Universal. He insisted there wasn't enough room on one show for two stars. Predictably, Burt's roles began to shrink. When he did get to do a scene, McGavin would try to psyche him out, whispering to him just before the cameras rolled how badly Burt was playing it, how backwards his approach was. Pretty soon Burt was walking around the set referring to himself as Dum Dum, the Whistle Blower. Pretty soon all he had left to do in the series was blow the whistle each time the riverboat left the dock.

Burt complained to the producers, reminding them his contract said he was the co-star. The studio, used to Hollywood actor temperament, countered Burt's complaints in typical fashion. They offered him a larger dressing room, then a shower in his dressing room, and what they figured would be the clincher, what, after all, every young Hollywood actor hankered for—a better parking space on the lot! Burt was so furious that the next time one of the associate directors made a comment to him he didn't like, he punched him in the jaw, sending him overboard the riverboat into the Mississippi-on-the-Universal.

It wasn't too long after that incident Burt and two other contract players were called into the executive offices at Universal to be told by Dick Irving their services were no longer required. Along with Burt were Clint Eastwood and David Janssen. Janssen was told he was being fired because of his "damn facial tic." Eastwood was informed that he had a chip on his tooth, his Adam's apple stuck out too far, and he talked too slow. As for Burt, he just didn't have any talent. Leaving the executive offices, Burt and Clint went for their cars, only to discover the names on their parking spaces were already being changed, Clu Gulager's neatly stenciled in over Burt's. Turning to Eastwood and smiling, Burt said, "I may learn to act some day but you'll never get rid of that Adam's apple. So there's no hope for you." They became close friends from that day on.

Burt was pretty much disgusted with the movie and TV business after "Riverboat." Even his love life was crazy. He'd met, fallen in love with, and became engaged to Lori Nelson, a "starlet" (contract player) who'd appeared in one "Riverboat" episode. Pretty, refined, popular, she perfectly fitted into the correct category, but their engagement promptly ended when he was fired, leaving a bitter taste in his mouth.

As did the garbage Universal was releasing to the press about how Burt "quit" the show. Was-

serman and Universal cautioned Burt to let the
story stand. The studio and MCA were anxious
to keep good relations with the new, ever-in-
creasing independent producers whom, it was obvious, were calling all the shots in town. Nobody
wanted bad press, his agents told him. If word
got out he'd been fired it could hurt his career, as
well as "Riverboat," the series barely hanging on
as it was. So the official story given to the press
was that Burt, quality actor, was seeking better
roles, looking for "new directions" in his career.
The gnawing anger in the pit of his stomach
started rising again as he heard echoes of his father calling him a "quitter." This time he hadn't
quit, he'd been fired, and he couldn't even set the
record straight. It wasn't long before the frustration drove him back to the Hollywood he knew
so well, the Hollywood of after-hours clubs,
places where the women were fast and cheap,
and meaningless.

All the time he'd been in Hollywood, the most
valuable lesson he'd learned had come on the
back lot of Universal, where he'd wandered
around during the day while "Riverboat" was
shooting, there being so little for him to do in
the show. Filming at Universal the same time as
"Riverboat" was the feature film INHERIT
THE WIND, starring Frederick March and
Spencer Tracy. Every day Burt found himself
back on the set of INHERIT THE WIND,
marveling at the ease with which Tracy handled
his part. One day, after shooting was completed,
Burt was leaning against the side of the sound-
stage when Tracy walked right up to him. "Who

are you, anyway?" Tracy asked. "Why are you
always hanging around here?"

"I'm an actor, sir," Burt replied. "My name's
Burt Reynolds." Tracy's face melted into a
warm, ruddy smile as he winked and said, softly,
"An actor, huh? Just remember not to let anyone catch you at it."

For a while it seemed as though that wouldn't
be a problem. For whatever the reason, either
the Brando thing or the bad reputation he'd gotten from "Riverboat," Burt just couldn't find
work as an actor. Very occasionally a syndicated
cheapie like "The Pony Express" would toss him
a small crumb, but soon it was back to falling
through windows, off horses, out second story
western hotel rooms, whatever the script called
for. It was during this period he kept running
into Hal Needham, a stunt man Burt had gotten
to know during "Riverboat," a guy who figured
Burt was okay. During the run of the series,
Needham had been assigned to do Burt's stunt
work. Burt, though, had insisted on doing all his
own stunts, making Needham's most strenuous
job picking up his retainer at the end of each
week's shooting. Now, when weeks could go by
with Burt not being able to find a single horse to
fall off of, Needham let him know there was always a place where he'd be welcome for a good
meal and a place to sleep. Maybe it was the way
they related to each other, these two tough,
hard-as-nails stunt men. Or the fact they were
both part Indian, Needham pulsing Blackfoot
blood in his veins. Whatever the reason, they

sensed a comraderie, cemented when Burt was told by Needham the door to his place was always open.

Stunting, though, wasn't what Burt wanted. He'd been a star, however briefly, in a series; now he couldn't buy his way onto Universal's tour. Finally, seeing no hope for a future in Hollywood, Burt packed his bags and headed back to New York, hoping to find acting work on Broadway.

six

THE following is a press release dated September 26, 1961:

WITH THE SIGNING OF TV ACTOR BURT REYNOLDS THE SIX-CHARACTER CAST OF THE NEW HUGH WHEELER PLAY, *Look, We've Come Through*, IS NOW COMPLETE. JOSE QUINTERO IS DIRECTING THE SAINT-SUBBER PRODUCTION WHICH OPENS OCTOBER 25 AT THE HUDSON AFTER A WEEK OF PREVIEWS. THE CAST ALSO INCLUDES COLLIN WILCOX, RALPH WILLIAMS, CLINTON KIMBROUGH, ZOHRA LAMPERT, AND ZACH MATALON.

MR. REYNOLDS BECAME ONE OF HOLLYWOOD'S MOST RESOLUTE REBELS TWO YEARS AGO WHEN HE WALKED OUT ON A CO-STARRING ROLE IN A NETWORK TV SHOW, "RIVERBOAT," BECAUSE HE WANTED TO "GROW AS AN ACTOR." SINCE THEN HE HAS PLAYED THE "HEAVY" ON EVERY MAJOR TV SHOW ON THE AIR FROM "ALFRED HITCHCOCK PRESENTS" TO "PONY EXPRESS". HE HAS APPEARED ONCE BEFORE ON THE NEW YORK STAGE IN THE 1957 CITY CEN-

TER REVIVAL OF *Mr. Roberts.* HE IS A NATIVE
OF PALM BEACH, FLORIDA AND ALUMNUS OF
FLORIDA STATE UNIVERSITY WHERE HE WAS
AN ALL-SOUTHERN AND ALL-STATE FOOTBALL
PLAYER.

It's hard to tell which was the greater work of
fiction, the play or the press release. There it was
in black and white, Burt "quitting" the show because he wanted to "grow," no mention of his
actual birthplace, Georgia (which would disap-
pear from practically all future interviews and
background articles, along with having lived in
poverty and the family tensions), and the impli-
cation that he'd graduated from Florida State
instead of dropping out, and of course, no mention at all of West Palm Beach Junior College.
Show-biz, folks.

LOOK! WE'VE COME THROUGH was
Burt's final appearance on Broadway, and a
wholly unsatisfying experience. The play closed
after five performances, sinking under its own
pretentious weight, taking with it, Burt's Broadway career. Now, there seemed little point in
continuing in New York. The only work he managed to get after LOOK! were two small roles in
independent feature films, both shot abroad. The
first, ANGEL BABY, also starred George Hamil-
ton, Mercedes McCambridge, Salome Jens and
Joan Blondell. It was never released theatrically
in the United States, getting only a small play-
off in England late in 1963. The other film, AR-
MORED COMMAND, starring Howard Keel,

Tina Louise, Earl Holliman, and Marty Ingels
was shot in Germany, where Burt was constantly
mistaken for Brando. One young woman even
came up to him on a German street and said,
"Mr. Brando, will you give me your autograph?"

"I'm not Mr. Brando," Burt said.

"I know you are."

"I'm not," Burt insisted, getting angry and
yelling, "Will you get away from me?" convincing the woman it definitely was Marlon Brando.
Who else had that attitude?

ARMORED COMMAND was a forgettable
war movie congested with meaningless dialogue
smothered in lots of combat. When each day's
shooting was completed, the actors hit the German bars with a vengeance. Burt got tight right
away with a barmaid in one of the nearby local
beer joints, who spoke little English to Burt's no
German. One night Burt brought Marty Ingels,
one of his co-stars, along with him, promising a
good time—lots of thick warm beer and easy
frauleins. Ingels, an up-and-coming comic actor
who would appear briefly in the comedy series
"I'm Dickens, He's Fenster" before starting his
own successful advertising agency in Hollywood,
was something of a ladies' man himself. The two
got loose quickly. The bars, for the most part,
accommodated the rowdy shenanigans of the actors the way postwar Germany had accommodated the real army during the occupation.

Things were flowing pretty smoothly for the
two until one night they picked the wrong bar.
Only a week earlier, an American soldier, a real
one, had killed a German civilian there in a fight.

While Ingels was refilling his mug at the bar, a couple of swollen-faced Germans surrounded him, pointing broken beer bottles at his face. Burt saw what was happening and without hesitating ran to one end of the bar, jumped on a table, leapt onto a hanging lamp, and swung like Tarzan into the three Germans, pulling it off no differently than any one of a hundred stunts he'd performed for TV and the movies. Taking the Germans by surprise, Burt knocked two of them out, leaving the third one, a six-foot-eight giant, dazed and angry. As he shook his head to regain his senses, a barmaid led Burt and Ingels to the icebox, letting them cool off until the police arrived. Today Ingels credits Burt with saving his life that night. By any account, this episode would have made a much better movie than ARMORED COMMAND, which was quickly released in America and quickly forgotten.

In 1962, Burt found himself back in Hollywood, ready to resume his career as a stuntman. Hanging out with his buddies Clint Eastwood and Hal Needham, Burt was always on the lookout for acting work. He was sent up to audition for a part in "Gunsmoke," television's *premiere* series. "You're too fat in the face to play an Indian," the producers told him after viewing his screentest, which Burt found kind of ironic. His response to them was typical Burt. Not only was he a real Indian, but if all they wanted was reality, they should go to Oklahoma. If they wanted an actor, they should let him know. Norman MacDonnell, one of the producers of "Gun-

smoke," was impressed and decided to go with
Burt, on a semi-regular basis, to play Quint As-
per, the half-breed blacksmith. It's always been
assumed that Burt was the replacement for Den-
nis Weaver, who, having limped through several
seasons of "Gunsmoke" decided to "branch out"
to look for "quality roles." Actually, Weaver
didn't leave the show until 1964, two years after Burt first appeared.

It was by far the biggest break Burt had gotten yet. "Gunsmoke" was an established hit, and
his role broad enough for him to play some
pretty meaty scenes. Burt describes this period
as the "happiest of my life." The producers and
directors were beginning to know him by name,
and the public was starting to recognize him. To
put it another way, he was still having trouble
getting tables, but in better restaurants. Fan
magazines began doing exaggerated "bios" on
Burt—6'2", 164 Lbs, and available, girls!

"What's your idea of the perfect woman,
Burt?"

"A unique combination of courtesan and
lady," he told one magazine.

(A couple of weeks later while he was in his
"Gunsmoke" trailer someone came knocking. He
opened the door to a very sexy young thing with
a copy of the magazine interview spread across
her cinemascope chest. "I'm her," she said coyly,
pointing to Burt's interview.)

CBS began sending Burt out on junkets
around the country to promote "Gunsmoke." In
those days, the networks insisted on personal appearance tours by the stars of the shows they

owned. It was on a CBS junket plane that Burt first laid eyes on the cute little fox with a nose upturned to heaven and a smile that smacked pornographic—Miss Judy Carne, star of the 1962 CBS sit-com, "Fair Exchange."

Judy Carne had been in America for only a few months when she met Burt. Riding the first ripples of what was to become the sixties' British Invasion of the entertainment world, she was quickly signed on to play for CBS the British daughter of a middle-class London family whose father agrees to swap daughters with his old American war-time buddy, now living in New York. The series, an hour long, very unusual for a situation comedy, was a total disaster. Yet, a lot of mail was generated when CBS announced it was canceling "Fair Exchange," prompting the network to revive it in mid-season, March 1963, in a half-hour format. The shorter version also failed, and after a summer of reruns the show was canceled, but not before CBS gave Judy the Personal Appearance junket tour of duty.

Junkets were arranged so that the stars of series would be flown into a city, collected in a hotel, do maybe a day at a shopping center or a hospital, or a school, then put on display in a large rented hall in a hotel. Here's the way Judy recalls meeting Burt: "The very first time I looked at him it was . . . all the way. That magical thing. It happens to you very rarely in life. Some people never experience it. He was sitting next to me on the CBS plane. The minute I spoke to him, the minute I looked at his face, I

knew, he knew, and I knew he knew. By the end
of the plane journey, if there wouldn't have been
anyone around, we would have been at it. As
soon as we got to the hotel where we were going
for the interviews, as soon as one of our interviews was over we'd rush into the first available
empty room. They'd tell us we had twenty
minutes or something. Of course we'd be together each night."

He was twenty-six years old, she twenty-two
when Judy was smitten by what Burt later
described as his "number three" virile look.
Their "friendship" on the junket was obvious to
everyone, providing for a lot of winking and
backslapping. When Burt and Judy returned to
Los Angeles, they spent most nights in Judy's
neat Hollywood efficiency; Burt's apartment always strewn with clothes and encrusted pots on
a filthy stove, being, as Judy remembers, a bit
too "ratty" for her tastes.

The first days of their relationship were one
long, happy laugh. Here, at last, for Burt was a
girl who thought he was funny as well as physical. "The first thing that struck me about Burt
was his magic, his sense of humor, how we never
stopped laughing." After only a few weeks, Burt
asked her to live with him.

They found a small house in the Hollywood
Hills on Mulholland Drive overlooking Los Angeles. One morning, over coffee, just before heading off to their respective sound stages, Burt
turned to Judy. "We're living together. We've
been living together for six months. Judy, I want
to marry you. I want us to be married."

"Burt, you don't have to marry me," Judy answered softly. "We're already living together."

"It's not good enough. I want you to be my wife. I want to refer to you as my wife." Logical enough for a southern boy whose family was already fearful the demons of Hollywood were swallowing up their boy. Burt knew it would please them. He was sure the move was right on all counts. After all, he felt on top of the world now. He was in a hit series, he was starting to get recognition, there was food on the table and someone next to him who smelled good in the morning.

They were married 1964, in a tiny Methodist church on Tojunga Avenue in the heart of Hollywood. "Neither of us were Methodist," Judy recalled, "but it was a pretty church and we thought a church wedding was the right thing to do. Hal Needham was there, so was Clint. We had a lovely little ceremony. My mother and father flew over from England, and Burt's parents were there." How proud Burt must have felt in front of his parents, especially his father. His mother hadn't told him about all the nights she would turn on "Gunsmoke," or any of the other shows he'd been in, only to have Burt Sr. come into the room and turn the set off. It was a big step for Burt to invite his father to the wedding; as big a step as it must have been for the chief to come to it.

For their honeymoon Burt wanted to drive up to Carmel. They decided to leave their parents in the Mulholland House and go immediately

to a little cabin they'd rented, close to where
Clint Eastwood lived. They arrived late in the
afternoon, as the sun began dipping into the
Pacific. If Judy was looking forward to a big
night, Burt was looking forward to an even bigger one. There was a hot football game on TV,
and Burt called Clint to ask if he was going to
watch it. Sure, come on over, Clint said. In a
flash, Burt and Judy were up at Clint's. The only
trouble was, Clint rarely watched television, so
he was as surprised as Burt to find out they
couldn't get the game because of interference
from the adjoining mountains. No problem, Burt
figured. They'd just all hop back into the car and
drive home to L.A. After all, this was a big
game.

The first year of their marriage was idyllic.
Lots of laughs, lots of good times. Burt even
made jokes about losing his hair. He would tell
Judy his hair problem was because he was half-
Italian and half-Indian. One half wanted to grow
hair, the other wanted to cut it off. Judy used to
tease him about his performance in "Gunsmoke"
by describing it in one word: muscles.

When her own series was cancelled, Burt was
very reassuring, telling Judy not to worry, she
would soon find something else, something better. In an attempt to cheer her up he gave her a
beautiful, black leather director's chair. Across
the back, it read, "Mrs. Burt Reynolds."

Mrs. Burt Reynolds tried at first to conform
to Burt's notion of what a wife, his wife, should

be. She tried to keep the house as he liked, not even suggesting a change of decor from the awful "early cowboy" style Burt seemed to love so much—lots of wooden chairs and stools, animal horns, and bear skin rugs. Oh, whatever it looked like, it didn't really matter, she told herself. It was their own private dream world.

Until the dream began to shatter. Judy wanted to cut her hair short. Burt insisted it was "unfeminine" for a woman to have short hair. He didn't like it when she wore trousers, preferring her in skirts and frilly blouses. And he hated the way she gushed and oozed over those ridiculous Beatles, the way she reminded Burt they were from England and how great it was over there, and . . . "Judy, you're a grown woman," Burt would remind her whenever she would get too carried away like that.

He would boast to her constantly about all the previous women in his life, all the conquests he'd made, the hearts he'd broken, filling her with every last detail. The unbroken rule, though, was that Judy could never under any circumstances even mention casually to him any man she'd known before him.

Things got worse when Burt was let go from "Gunsmoke." Two and a half seasons had been enough for the producers. They wanted, as they put it, "new directions." Two actors out of work in the same house is difficult under the best of circumstances. Between Burt and Judy, it was a disaster.

Judy had an opportunity to get work first, in a

series called "The Baileys of Balboa." The part
called for Judy to play the daughter of a pomp-
ous Commodore (John Dehner) who doesn't
get along with his neighbor, a simple, unpreten-
tious widower (Paul Ford) who runs a small
charter fishing boat whose son falls in love with
the Commodore's daughter, who's in love with
bla bla bla. Judy was perfect for the part, except
for her British accent. As the daughter of an un-
pretentious lunatic she had to play, and sound,
all-American whacko. Burt announced to Judy
that he could teach her how to speak like a native. He worked with her day and night, drilling
her phonetically, training her like a coach with a
new kid for the team, becoming obsessed with
breaking her accent. He convinced, and petrified,
Judy with the idea that American producers
were all morons, that if she walked in to the audition with a British accent she could sound like
Lady Bird Johnson during her scene and
wouldn't get the part. No, Burt insisted, she'd
have to sound completely American. By the time
she took the audition there wasn't a trace of an
accent, and she got the part.

Then, according to Judy, something strange
happened. After working so hard to help her,
Burt started talking about having children. He
was convinced they should have a baby, that he
wanted to be a father. Sure, Judy said, sure,
Burt, but not right now. We've got plenty of
time for that. Once it became clear to Burt that
Judy was going to take the series over mother-
hood, he became morose, stand-offish; grumpy if

he bothered to get up at six in the morning when she had to leave for the studio, cranky at seven in the evening when she'd return at night. She tried to play homemaker in spite of her impossible schedule. According to Judy, "I would go to work, do my scenes, market on the way home, cook dinner for Burt, clean the house, make sure he had clean shirts. But the more I pulled it off, the more crazed he got, and the more insecure."

Money was another problem for them. Judy was earning $200,000 a year, while Burt was making nothing except occasional residuals. Still, they bought a new house on Laurel Crescent Drive on the other side of the Hollywood Hills, the side that faces the valley, closer to the studios, cutting her travel time down a bit. She hoped the new house would give Burt something to do; fix it up, turn it into another Roy Rogers ranch if he liked, she really didn't care. Instead, as Judy tells it, "Burt started fantasizing I was screwing everybody around. I would come in at night from work and he would say, 'Well, who did you screw today? I know what film sets are like when an attractive girl is around, you know.' He would sit and have these black moods. He would sit, with all the drapes closed all day. And he would stare, his head down, hours and hours and hours in deep concentration."

There were very few people who could reach him. Hal Needham was one. Clint Eastwood was another. Clint brought over a script he'd been sent by an Italian director. "It's something called a spaghetti western," Eastwood told Burt.

"Rawhide" was still on the network and summer
hiatus was coming up, a two-to-three month
break from shooting. "It's called A FISTFUL
OF DOLLARS. There's not much money involved but I could shoot the whole thing during
hiatus."

"Do it," Burt advised him. "What have you
got to lose?" It probably didn't help matters any
for Burt when the film, released only months
later, turned Eastwood into a major international superstar. Besides getting into a spaghetti
westerns, Eastwood had also gotten into TM
(Transcendental Meditation). Eastwood tried
his best to get Burt into it, convinced it would
help him, and Burt did give it half a try. Then,
as now, Clint loved Burt as one of the boys, and
hated to see him so depressed.

While Burt "meditated" in his chair, Judy
tried her best to cope. "I felt for him so much. I
tried never to bring up the fact that I was the
so-called breadwinner. I knew it was just a question of time. . . . It was so obvious with his
kind of personality, he had everything going for
him. I knew he would make it sooner or later. It
was inevitable."

If his success seemed inevitable, so was something else.

"He started to get violent. Out of insecurity
he'd lash out. He really and truly didn't know
what he was doing. He would get into such a
rage that he really wouldn't know what he was
doing. Afterwards he'd almost cry and beg for-
giveness, and I would forget it. It started with

pushes and slaps. As things got worse and his depressions deepened, it was very painful."

Burt began suspecting Judy of being with other men, although she assured him she had no desire for anyone but him. Out of desperation one day she bought a punching bag as a present for Burt. "It worked for a while, but then the focus came back to me." Understandably, Judy began dreading the return home each night after a tough day at the studio. "If I came home and saw his car in the garage and the curtains drawn, I knew right away Burt was having a "black" day. So I would sort of creep in. I was terrified of him. Mortified. I was afraid of my own safety. His first words would be, 'Who did you screw today?' and he'd be off. 'I called the studio, I know what time you left.' If I told Burt I'd run into an old friend, he'd be sure I'd had a quick affair. He got so angry one time he picked me up and threw me. I went screaming from the house for help, begging my neighbor to save me."

Judy was badly bruised, and in shock. Her neighbor took her to the nearest hospital where she was rushed to the emergency room for treatment, then admitted overnight for observation. "The following day I called him and threatened divorce. Now I never, never wanted a divorce. More than that I never dreamt that Burt would take me up on it. All he could say was, 'If that's what you want. . . .'

" 'If that's what I want . . . what I want, Burt, is to be safe. Not to live in fear. I want to be with you, to have a happy marriage.' "

Burt's answer came slowly. "I'm sitting in the chair, waiting for you to come back."

She called the next day and got the same answer. "So I contacted a lawyer. He got through to Burt and got the same response. All this time I thought, Oh God, he'll change his mind, he'll come around. But he didn't, and no one was more shocked than I was. My threat was followed up, and followed through. I remember walking up the steps to the courthouse to get the divorce I still had the feeling that he would suddenly jump out and come around. I don't know why, really. He couldn't make that step."

Burt was sitting in the house, shattered.

Finally, terrifyingly, he reached for the telephone to call his mother. "Tell dad he was right about me. Tell him I'm a quitter." Once he started, he couldn't stop. The words spilled out of him; everything, everywhere. He'd run away from home because he hadn't been able to take it. He was a failure at school, a failure in two TV series, he couldn't hold a steady job, and now he couldn't even hold on to his wife. A failure.

"Come on home." The words came back to him through the receiver in the steady, measured tones of Burt, Sr. "Come on home. I'll tell you about all the things I've quit in my life."

Burt caught the first plane home. At the airport he threw his arms around his father and hugged him for the first time in his life. Throughout that night, in the elastic tropical heat, Burt and his dad talked it all over, passing a bottle of cognac back and forth like a peace pipe.

. . . *There is an unspoken rule in the South between a father and his son: You ain't a man until your father tell you you're a man.*

seven

EARNING acceptance from his father was what it was all about. That had had to come before Burt could begin to accept himself. He knew that now. He knew now it was time to change his attitude. If his disastrous marriage to Judy had taught him anything, it was that he had to let go of his "why-me" self-pity in favor of the "why-not-me" bravado lurking inside trying to punch its way to daylight. He was down now, but he was tough, he'd proven that. He could take a punch and come back swinging. He'd been saved by the bell, he was back in his own corner, bruised ego being sponged down by the chief. Okay. Square things and then on with it, that was the order of the day.

He wanted his father to retire, to hang up the badge. He'd served the community long enough. Burt wanted to give his dad a gift of some land, a place the old man could build on; a physical bond to confirm the emotional one. Along with a couple of investment partners, including Jim Kimberly of Kimberly-Clark, Burt purchased 180 acres of land in Jupiter, Florida, tobacco-spitting distance from the right side of the tracks. It was the first major investment for Burt, the first sensible thing he'd done with the money he'd made from "Gunsmoke," and what better way to spend it than on a dream, Burt personally drew up an intricate set of construction plans for his father to work from. Lots of open space, plenty of housing for the family and staff, and a special, private tree house for Burt. If he was going to go out on a limb, he might as well do it in style.

Originally built in 1923, the ranch belonged to Al Capone who used it as a hideout for himself and the boys whenever things got too hot in Chicago. Burt, Sr. lost no time face-lifting the weedy land; knocking down walls and fences and killing rattlesnakes. Burt Jr., on hand for the start of the long restoration, promised to return often to watch, with pride, the construction of his personal monument to self-worth.

No sooner did Burt arrive in New York—he wasn't anxious to return to Hollywood quite yet—than reporters were on him for a comment about his well-publicized divorce. Finally, he issued a general statement which he would repeat whenever asked. Burt's explanation for what went wrong: "I'd call it a good marriage that didn't work." Judy's explanation was even better. Being interviewed all over the place, and loving it, her responses were well-prepared and well-performed. Question: Did Burt give you a decent settlement? Answer: I didn't want anything. Question: Didn't you get the house? I bought out Burt's half. Question: Was it sex, was sex a problem?

Sex? That was no problem. Burt was FAN-TASTIC in bed. I can heartily recommend him.

Question: Then, what exactly was it?

Burt was right wing and I was left wing. The problem was political. You know how that can be.

"I understand you play a lot of Indians," Dino De Laurentiis said, huddling with Burt over drinks and a script. NAVAJO JOE seemed like a natural to De Laurentiis. It seemed like a zillion other spaghetti western scripts, to Burt—starchy plot, minimal dialogue for easy dubbing into every language in the universe, lots of bullets and TNT, twangy schlock-rock score for the kids, fancy camera flow for the film freaks, and death, lots of death. Plot: Navajo Joe thins out the entire white population on behalf of the buffalo; something Indian like that.

De Laurentiis was being very persuasive. A FISTFUL OF DOLLARS, need he remind Burt, had made his pal Clint an international star as the man with no name who killed 53 guys in one movie. Well, ol' Navajo could kill 115 in the first hour, no sweat! It was quick, it was action, it was Spain, it was money. And, as Burt would add later, it was the worst movie he'd ever made, maybe the worst movie ever made, period. "So awful," he told anyone who asked, "It was shown only in prisons and airplanes because no-body could leave. I killed 10,000 guys, wore a Japanese slingshot and a fright wig."

Burt returned to New York as soon as the last stick of TNT had been tossed, convinced that Sergio "You gonna kill-a a hondred-a guy-a the first five minoots" Corbucci's films would never, under any circumstances, be confused with director Sergio Leone of FISTFUL fame.

With international stardom on hold, Burt agreed to a meeting with Paul Bogart, a producer from Screen Gems which, with ABC, was interested in Burt for a new TV series, "Hawk." Burt had sworn, after "Gunsmoke," he'd never do another series, but he had to admit, this offer was tempting. He'd play a present-day New York detective; acting in the twentieth century was a novelty for Burt. The series would be shot on location, in New York. He'd be the star; no holding horses or tooting whistles. Being the star thrilled him. That Hawk happened to be an Indian didn't. The hook, the twist, the producers insisted, would be that Hawk, a modern Indian, stalked criminals by "natural Indian instinct" down the bad streets of New York City.

Burt agreed to do the series if they'd tone down the Indian bits. No headdresses, those were definitely out. No "ums"—"You look-um in alley, I take-um front door." While Burt may have thought the network was eager to build a show around him, happy to accede to his demands, the fact was almost entirely opposite. Burt was perfect for "Hawk" precisely because he wasn't a star. Being familiar but not outstanding, he was the face needed to fill the slot, and the slot was all the network cared about.

"Hawk" would never have been made if not

for the highly popular NBC series "I Spy," begun a season earlier and hitting ratings gold mix-
ing black with white in the one-two punch of Bill
Cosby and Robert Culp. As "I Spy" nestled in
the Top Ten, the word went out from rival ABC
to Screen Gems, it wanted this year's "I Spy."
The crucial elements required by the network
were lots of location shooting, simple, appealing
detective stuff plot-wise, and most important,
that same chemistry between Culp and Cosby.
In typical network rationale, if "I Spy" worked
because of one minority, a Black, the first Black
star of a network show since the days of "Amos
'n' Andy," think what two minorities could do; a
Black and an Indian!

A year can be an eternity in television. While
Cosby's 1965 character in "I Spy was popular,
he was still highly regulated and restricted; a
colorless Rhodes scholar. Hawk's 1966 Black
partner, played by Wayne Grice, would be hip.
Hip Blacks were in now. Cosby had crawled,
Grice could strut. Indians? Most Indians don't
have TV's. Hawk was Tonto as far as the network was concerned. They wanted Burt to wear
knives up his sleeves, maybe have him prowl
around in Manhattan in moccasins with his ear
to the street listening for approaching stolen
cars, who cared? Hadn't Cosby walked away
with all the emmys last year while Culp had
been the spy left out?

There was tension on the set, but not between
Burt and Grice. Burt went out of his way to
make sure Grice didn't go through his own version of "Riverboat." The tension was between

Burt and the producers. Burt constantly demanded better, more believable scripts; a general loosening up of Hawk's character. Throughout the long shooting days, Burt would find himself tightening up inside, getting more and more frustrated. Hitting the New York bars at night, he found the New York women as aggressive and available as ever, the perfect complement to the fifth-a-day he was drinking and the "appetite-depressant" pills he was taking to lose some of that stubborn chubbiness. The producers were constantly on him to lose weight so his cheekbones would be more prominent; more ... Indian.

"Hawk" debuted Thursday, September 8, 1966 at ten o'clock on ABC, opposite the long running "CBS Thursday Night Movies," and NBC's sloshy but popular "Dean Martin Show." A quick glance at "Hawk's" placement in the prime-time schedule brought snickers from the programming boys at the other networks. No problem here. "Hawk" was bound for the Nielsen happy hunting ground.

The New York Times agreed: " 'HAWK,' which opened last night on ABC was too shrill and intense to be entirely winning." As for the plot, *The Times* described it as a story "with a religious psychotic of topical and different turn. The murderer was motivated by protest against the age of automation after he had lost his elevator job. In his demented desperation he dials a telephone number to obtain solace and is rewarded with only a recorded player." Burt? "Reynolds playing an Indian working as a detec-

tive . . . needs to loosen up in his acting and
not be quite so stern."

He'd been right all along, he told the producers, Hawk had to loosen up. Even if he'd
been able to convince him he was right, which he
didn't, there were already eight episodes in the
can, and there was nothing anybody could do
about those. It finally didn't matter one way or
another, because ABC canceled "Hawk" after
only five weeks, making it the second fatality of
the '66-'67 season (the first being "The Tammy
Grimes Show"). "Hawk" placed ninth from the
bottom of the Nielsen ratings with a weak 12.7
share, meaning approximately twelve sets out of
every hundred on watched "Hawk." With three
major networks, survival requires a minimum
one third, or 30 share.

They were on location when the hatchet fell.
It was nighttime, lower Broadway. The mood on
the set was less than gleeful. Still, they had an
episode to finish. This one called for a "dead
body" to be found lying in the street. Just as
they were getting ready to roll, a slightly tipsy,
middle-aged woman came strolling by. Spying
the "dead body" lying right there on Broadway,
she froze in horror. Then, gingerly, she approached it, bent down, and clutched it to her
bosom, stroking its head, murmuring over and
over not to worry, everything would be all right.
A couple of crew members comforted the
woman, trying to get her to let go of the "body."
The woman, though, was determined to hang in
there. A mini-battle ensued; even the dead body
got involved. It was far easier for Burt to walk

away from the dead series than it was to get that woman off the dead "body."

So much for "Hawk." Burt's final words to the producers were to the effect that they'd capitalized on the wrong half of his heritage. They should have made "Hawk" Italian, the owner of a pizza parlor, possessing a natural instinct for making calzone. Burt swore, again, he'd never do another TV series as long as he lived.

eight

NEVERTHELESS, Burt declared, 1966 had been the happiest year of his life. Hey, Burt seemed to be shouting at the top of his lungs, I'm happy, goddamnit!

In fact, as 1967 came creeping over the cold New York skyline a thirty-two-year-old Burt Reynolds was looking for work. With nothing happening on the East Coast, Burt felt it was time at last to return to Hollywood. He'd moved his things to Hal Needham's place when he'd broken up with Judy; Needham was happy to have Burt crash there until he got his bearings. With some hustling, and some compromising, Burt managed to get a couple of films. Paramount gave him one, so did United Artists; as long as they could call the shots.

The pictures were fast and furious. RENE-GADES, FADE-IN, SAM WHISKEY, 100 RIFLES, IMPASSE. Burt was pulling down about $150,000 a pop, conforming to the requisite formula of action, and bare chest. Any given day could find him having a fist fight, having the girl, having a drink and having a re-take. It got to the point that on the rare day he'd find himself off a set, near a real swimming pool, he'd wait for someone to yell "cut" as he dove in.

As far as Burt was concerned, the films and the roles were interchangeable. He could be an Indian, he might be a stuntman, a cowboy, or a detective, it didn't matter. He always got the girl. Whether it was in Hollywood, on location in Colorado, somewhere in Europe or Asia, on the moon if they could get a permit, by the end of the first reel, Burt had bedded the leading lady, and almost as many times off-screen as on. Along the way he began to understand how the movie business really worked. For example, it became clear to him early on that no one cared about actors or directors. Producers held all the power and cared about one thing—money. The bottom line.

He'd gotten a taste of this with "Hawk." Once the show was canceled, the producers quickly lost interest. What's that, Burt, you want to write an episode? No problem. You want to direct? Take the last two episodes, Buddy, have a ball. Burt was sure the reason "Hawk" had failed was because the producers had been so busy thinking headdress they'd missed the feather in their cap. "Hawk" should have had a girl friend. Even in films as mindless as IM-PASSE (which Burt would later say brought his career to an impasse), the first thirty minutes would return the investment because Burt was in and out of bed every two seconds with a chick. Given the chance to produce, he'd know what to do. He'd exploit the Burt Reynolds character the way he knew it could be exploited, using women the way all the great male stars did—as proof of their charisma, the stamp of their heroic attitudes, the ace of their hearts. If only he could get the chance.

Meanwhile, off-screen, Burt was collecting women like arrowheads. It came to a point, Burt would tell *Playboy* years later, when he'd have trouble remembering who was next to him when he woke up in the morning, sometimes even how she got there.

Until he met Miko. Miko Mayama, a Japanese actress starring in the TV series, "The Hawaiians," was the first woman Burt felt something for since Judy.

Burt and Miko were seen everywhere. He insisted they move in together. He got his things from Needham's place and moved them into a big, new house. Things were different now. He didn't feel subordinated by Miko, the way he'd felt with Judy; forced into the dark brooding background of her cockney effervescence. Burt totally dominated Miko. Oh, he might hint at marriage occasionally, but for Burt the edge of commitment was where the real action was. Marriage, that was the penalty for getting too close.

By the end of 1968 Burt had five pictures in the can and none in release. He dubbed himself the most popular unknown in Hollywood. He was banking on the steady, successful release of the films to build up enough muscle so that when the right time came, he'd be able to produce some movies of his own.

As they gradually reached the screen, though, his films were greeted with less than critical yahoos, and none were box-office blockbusters. Burt played cool, keeping himself at a distance, letting it be known he didn't consider any of these films classics. His comment on 100 RIFLES: "I was playing opposite Lunt and Fontanne. I mean Jim Brown and Raquel Welch." His opinion of Raquel Welch was not exactly the greatest.

Burt continued stockpiling movies, fast and furious, and for the most part forgettable. He was still looking for that one elusive killer film that would make him bankable; wounding himself along the way. He turned down M*A*S*H in favor of that all-time classic, SKULLDUGGERY. He refused to take over the James Bond role from Sean Connery, even though the money would have been fantastic. He wasn't interested in being anyone's replacement; he was an original, unique, not the next Sean Connery anymore than the next Marlon Brando. In fact, as he told one reporter, it was about time someone went up to Brando and asked him if he was Burt Reynolds! Anyway, Burt chuckled, even Brando didn't look like Brando anymore.

By his own admission, 1970 was the low point of his movie career. There just wasn't anything happening for him. In one of his who-cares-anymore moods, he accepted an invitation to appear on "The Dating Game," a game-show on the same network dangling a couple of made-for-TV movies in front of him. "The Dat-

ing Game" experience may have been a totally
humiliating one for Burt, and yet he picked up
on something about appearing on "live" TV.
Ironically, "The Dating Game" appearance, easily the low point of his professional career, would
prove to be a crucial experience for him a little
later on down the line.

"The Dating Game" was sexual fantasy
lobotomized for television. One woman, or "gal,"
as smiling host Jim Lang would refer to them,
would sit on a tall bar stool, often wearing a
clinging short dress with high heels; maybe the
itty bitty tips of her stockings sneaking out for
a second for all the world to see. Her hair fre-
quently bomb-struck-blonde, sprayed to paral-
ysis, her lips drowned in gloss, and her brain,
filled with "cute" double-entendre questions to
ask the three happy hopefuls behind the curtain. The curtain, prevented her from seeing,
and allowed her to only hear the clues from
which to choose her dream date.

This particular day, the blonde happened to
be a Hollywood starlet, and one of the three eli-
gible bachelors happened to be Burt Reynolds!
Could America stand the suspense?

The starlet was Christine Schmidler, whose
claim to fame was a small role in the Hollywood neo-classic, SHIP OF FOOLS. Behind
the curtain with Burt were Lee Grosscup,
one-time quarterback for the New York Football Giants, and Harvey Miller, a then unknown
comedy writer, who would one day go on to
write and co-produce PRIVATE BENJAMIN

with Goldie Hawn, and get nominated for an oscar. One day. This day he was grateful for the quick $750 all the panelists, including Burt, received and maybe a chance to score.

Showtime. Lang introduced Christine to the audience and the panel. "Say hello, bachelor number one." Grosscup, bachelor number one, grunted back a hello as if he were calling signals on third and ten. "Bachelor number two?" Miller, having been stationed in Germany while in the army, and picking up on the fact that Schmidler had a German accent, shouted, "Guten Tag, mein fraulein, wie geht's?" Christine bubbled over like warm champagne, while Lang chuckled monotonously. Bachelor number three, Burt, hello'd like he couldn't care less.

The clever questions. "Bachelor number three, what would you do if you and I were driving along and suddenly your tire went flat?"

"I'd fix you first, then the tire, ha-aaa. . . ." The audience erupted, but Burt's laugh was cleverly clipped by bachelor number two, Harvey, who turned on Burt and shouted, "How dare you talk to my date like that!" Still not through, Harvey turned in the direction of the curtain and told Lang, "I want to lodge a formal complaint!" The audience loved it, but Burt was fuming. Grosscup, meanwhile, was still trying to figure out how to play. "Bachelor number one, describe bachelor number two."

Grosscup: "That's a good question."

"Thank you. Bachelor number two, the same question, can you describe bachelor number three?"

Harvey was in hog heaven. "Let me put it this
way. Hitler is not in Argentina, he's sitting next
to me." Burt squirmed so much Harvey was
afraid to look directly at him. If he had, he
might have seen Burt's Fu Manchu mustache almost completely upside down, the result of his
face being twisted with anger.

Commercial.

"And now, it's time for our date to choose her
bachelor," Lang announced when they came
back, for the billionth time in his life, the thick
creases in his daytime TV smile holding the rest
of his face for ransom. Surprise, surprise, Christine chose bachelor number two. The audience
roared. He may have made a joke out of the
other two, but the final joke was on her.

". . . And here are the bachelors you didn't
choose. Bachelor number one is a professional
football player. Meet the quarterback of the
New York Giants, Lee Grosscup!" Christine's
eyes got a little dewy as the gentle giant thun-
dered from behind the curtain.

". . . And, Christine, had you chosen
bachelor number three, you would have gone on
the dream date of your life with movie star Burt
Reynolds! Pandemonium reigned throughout female America. She didn't get him! Burt, self-effacing to the end, smiling with eyes almost
completely closed, trotted around the curtain
with a so-what toss of his hand to the now-fren-
zied audience, and a this-could-have-been-yours
look for Christine. And Christine knew it, her
smile shrinking into desperation. Her last, faint
hope that bachelor number two would somehow

top what she passed up began to shatter when
Lang introduced Harvey as "Woody Al-
lenesque." Harvey came around the curtain and
was greeted by the back of Christine's head, her
eyes searching off-stage, behind her, for Burt.
Harvey tried to salvage the moment by declaring
to the audience that it was a great day for the
little guy before he, Lang, and Christine threw a
kiss to the audience, ending the show.

Backstage, though, there was a little epilogue.
Burt had Harvey against the wall, friendly, letting him know, though, that if the curtain had
been a glass window, Harvey wouldn't have
stood a chance. Harvey sweated out Burt's anal-
ysis hoping he'd forgotten the Hitler line. After
signing a release, Harvey finally got to meet
Christine who scribbled her service number on a
piece of paper for him to call to arrange the date
which, of course, never took place. Last seen,
Christine was backstage, chasing after Burt, ordering the security guards not to let him leave
the building.

It was a nightmare, but it taught Burt something. Things had certainly changed since his
days of live, New York TV. Since the days of
"Hawk." There was a reason the audience had
loved Harvey Miller, and it had nothing to do
with looks. Harvey knew how to "play" Harvey,
regardless of how calculated it may have been.
That was what Burt had been trying to get the
producers of "Hawk" to understand. No one
cared about some dumb Indian; it was Burt the
audience wanted. If he could only find a way to

project his "thing," his drink and babe in one hand, he could have any audience eating out of the other. What he needed now was a vehicle that would allow him to "play" Burt Reynolds.

So he didn't say no when one of the TV movies he did for ABC caught the attention of Quinn Martin, who wanted to talk to Burt about a new series. Quinn Martin, in 1970, was an important producer in television. His series, "The Fugitive," had made a star out of David Janssen, that fellow with the tic. Look, Quinn Martin told Burt, here's an idea that can't miss. You see, there's this detective. . . .

nine

"I'LL play anything but a cop," Burt told Quinn Martin. A cop, though, was exactly what Martin had in mind. He was sure that, handled correctly, Reynolds' blend of toughness and togetherness could make him the biggest thing in television. He offered him a unique deal, willing to match the highest paid actor's salary in television on a per-show basis if Reynolds would play a cop. Suddenly, for $20,000, Burt was dying to play Dan August. It was, he admitted, a complete sellout on his part.

Martin was willing to spend big. He needed a hit as badly as Reynolds did. "The Fugitive" had gone off the air in 1968, and he hadn't hit with anything quite as big since. He was hoping "Dan August" would do it for both Burt and himself. As for Burt, he was hoping for three good seasons out of "August," which would mean enough episodes for syndication and financial security for life. With money no problem and exposure for years on the tube, it would be simple to take control of his pictures, to finally make a Burt Reynolds movie.

He had enough respect for Martin not to fight

him every inch of the way, but to let the producer produce. A black secretary for Dan August, good move; a Mexican-American assistant,
sounds great. Burt went so far to try to cooper-
ate with Martin, he even wrote a column for the
Los Angeles Herald Examiner in August of
1970 with the unbelievable heading, "POLICE-
MEN NEED LOVE TOO":

> My nephew doesn't call me Uncle Burt any-
> more, he now calls me "Super Pig." It's a
> standing joke in our family and it refers to
> the fact that I play police detective Dan
> August in Quinn Martin's new ABC-TV
> series of the same name debuting this Sep-
> tember. . . . My responsibility to my
> personal principles, not only as an actor but
> also as a citizen, must therefore be reflected
> in the decisions I make as an actor, and it
> occurs to me that the polarization of the
> diverse ideologies in our society has reached
> such a critical stage that the future of our
> country is literally in danger.

Good thing "Dan August" was going to be
around! Burt really wanted this series to go!
Then, at the end, a curious reference to the real
policeman of the family, the man with the
loaded guns, Burt, Sr.

> Perhaps, because of my father, I honestly
> believe that in real life the vast majority of
> policemen are the kind of men that Dan
> August is in our series.

"Dan August" lasted twenty-six episodes. Ultimately, the Reynolds-Martin partnership had been a bad one. Martin's concept of August was lean and tough, humorless, flat-toned, interior. August rarely spoke more than a sentence at a time. None of Burt's bare-chest womanizer with a wisecrack of gold shone through, in spite of the $300,000 an episode Martin spent on the series. By the time it was over, Burt knew he'd made a mistake playing another cop, and playing him straight.

Now what? Burt took the first thing offered, a TV movie, "Run, Simon, Run," totally forgettable except for the fact that he fell in love with his co-star, Inger Stevens.

The Swedish beauty started the heat flowing through his veins again. Even though he was still involved with Miko, he plunged into a relationship with Inger in typical Reynolds fashion—constant, loving attention, public wining and dining, lavish gifts, extravagant courtliness. As for Miko, well, four years was a long time for Burt to stay with one woman. It was as long a time as he'd known Judy, from the first day on the plane to the last day in divorce court. Anyway, Miko had no choice. She could take it or she could leave it. She chose to take it, waiting silently for him, at home, if and when he cared to show up.

Some of Burt's friends felt he might ask Inger Stevens to marry him. What nobody knew, apparently, was that the lovely lady was already married, a secret so well kept it would be the major revelation at the probation of her will. At

the height of her love affair with Burt Reynolds,
Inger Stevens, for no apparent reason, killed herself.

Her death shocked Hollywood. She'd seemed
so happy, so dignified, so above the tawdry tinsel
tactics so much a part of the business. What no
one had been aware of were the incredible
pressures Stevens functioned under, brought
about by her romance and marriage to a black
man, still unacceptable in Hollywood in the late
sixties. Things hadn't changed all that much
since the fifties when another Swedish beauty,
May Britt, married Sammy Davis Jr., effectively
ending her career, nearly bringing down his.
Even while Stevens' hit TV series, "The Farm-
er's Daughter," was airing in the middle sixties,
headlines in newspapers were reporting the
"scandalous" physical contact broadcast on TV
between Harry Belafonte and Petula Clark, on
Belafonte's 1968 Christmas special. A momen-
tary touching of Clark's arm by Belafonte had
sent shock waves through America.

So all the while her series ran, and throughout
her working days in Hollywood, up to and including RUN, SIMON, RUN, Inger Stevens led
two lives—one public, happy, liberated; another
private, fearful, secretive. Then, to complicate
matters further, she fell in love with Burt Reynolds.

There is no doubt Burt knew she was married.
In fact, Burt, Inger Stevens and her husband
were all friends, often getting together socially.
There are those who believe that at one point
Inger Stevens decided she'd had enough of her

double life, that she was going to leave her husband for Burt, only to be rejected by Reynolds who feared getting involved any deeper; an involvement which, for the first time, could lead to a deeper commitment, even marriage if he wasn't careful. Her wrecked marriage, her rejection by Burt, and the collective pressures of balancing her career in the midst of her own personal problems brought her to the murky depths of an inescapable depression, relieved finally, by suicide. Her untimely death tossed Burt, in confused grief, back to Miko's waiting arms.

Not long after, Burt accepted an offer from Merv Griffen to appear on his talk show. He'd been approached by Merv and others before and had always refused. Even Dinah Shore's people had made overtures, calling constantly during the days of DAN AUGUST, hoping to get Burt to appear on Dinah's popular daytime cooking show. His continual refusals of Dinah's invitations became a joke around her show. First he would accept, then cancel out for some reason or another, always at the last minute. Maybe he needed something to do, maybe he wanted to test out what he'd learned from his DATING GAME experience, but whatever the reason, when Griffen's office called this time, he decided to give it a whirl.

The first thing Burt did on Merv's show, after crossing his legs and pretending to loosen his too-tight collar was to announce his unique distinction of having appeared on TV series that

had been canceled from all three networks.
Merv, sensing a live one, started asking the
kinds of question only Merv asks. Leaning over
in his chair, his face grinning like a wet wood-
pecker's in a pine tree, asked Burt if it was true
he had mirrors on his ceilings. Yes, Burt grinned,
it was true. Why, Merv wanted to know. Why?
Are you kidding!?!? "So when I wake up in the
morning I can see the person I love most." The
audience laughed at that line, but roared at the
next, as Burt's face spread into his handsome,
most self-effacing smile. "And if you believe
that, Merv, I've got some swamp land I'd like to
sell you."

That was it. Like a fat man after a big meal,
Merv sighed, sat back and smiled. Inside Burt's
tight pants, behind the clenched jaw and under
the curly toupee was one of us, America, just another regular guy. Burt talked, and talked and
talked, happily shooting the breeze like the good
ol' boy he just wished everybody knew he really
was.

It was quite a performance, Burt on Burt, and
Merv gave it a rave. He brought him back
eleven times in a row, breaking the previous
record for consecutive appearances that had belonged to Richard Pryor at seven. Before long,
Burt was asking Merv if he could maybe host
the show sometime. Sure, Merv told him, as
soon as he was ready he'd get a shot. What he
needed, first, was a little more experience. No
problem. Almost immediately, he got Dinah's
people on the phone. Were they still interested
in him for her show? Great. He'd do it, if they

could do something for him. Anything, they said. Okay, build a breakaway cooking table, don't tell Dinah, and hide me in her supply closet. I want to surprise her on the air.

Anything you say, Burt.

It happened when Dinah went for some mustard. Smiling, she opened her supply closet and pulled out Burt Reynolds. She was stunned, the audience roared. And that was only the beginning. Burt carried on like a lunatic, nonstop, for two hours, most of the material totally unusable for the show, eventually edited down to a barely salvageable fifteen minutes. All during the show, Burt outrageously flirted with Dinah, asking her again and again if she would go to Palm Springs with him for the weekend. "No," she repeatedly told him, flustered and flattered. Burt refused to take no for an answer. Finally, turning sullen, he told her. "Okay, then I'm going to kill myself." With that, he dove, head-first, onto her cooking table, which collapsed in a breakaway heap, sending food flying everywhere; a climactic melee the Three Stooges would have been proud of.

It continued backstage. Burt and Dinah laughed about the show, and promised to see each other again, soon. Returning home that night to Miko, Burt knew it was finally, irrevocably, over. Wasting no time, he came right to the point.

Surprisingly, to Burt, Miko was rather cool about it. He insisted she tell him what she wanted for the time she'd spent with him. She

told him she'd like a car, an apartment in
Malibu, and a few hundred dollars a week. It
was more than he'd bargained for. As he told
Playboy Magazine, "I figured she'd settle for
some record albums." Nevertheless, he agreed to
her terms, and Miko was out, leaving Burt free
to begin in earnest his pursuit of the aging singer
seventeen years his senior, a romance that would
cause a sensation in Hollywood and raise eye-
brows around the world.

ten

WHY Dinah? What was it about the fifty-two-year-old World War Two swing band vocalist that so captivated the thirty-five-year-old swinging bachelor? Was it her striking phy ical resemblance to Inger Stevens? Was Dinah's age a safety factor that would insure her loyalty and faithfulness, factors which had so obsessed Burt in his marriage? Had Stevens' untimely death caused those insecurities to re-surface? Did Burt feel safe from the threat of marriage because twice-divorced Dinah was probably as aisle-shy as he was?

Or was it something deeper, some final psychological smudge still to be laundered from Burt's subconscious; an emotional spot left over from the days when Buddy lived in Burt Sr.'s shadow. Dinah was, after all, the first American girl in a long time he'd gotten serious with—Judy was British, Miko Japanese, Stevens Swedish. Dinah, at last, was all-American. Southern, in fact, just like that gal "that married dear old dad." The Oedipal overtones necessarily come along with the Southern territory, and the peculiar age disparity. Had Burt finally found a way to relate to Burt, Sr. on the ultimate man-to-man level, by the woman he chose? Was there something left unresolved in Buddy's head, some remaining sliver of competitive rage still to be worked out? After all, Burt's attempts at playing stylized, movie versions of Indians and cops were, in a sense, competitive with his dad, a real-life Indian and an authentic cop. That Burt continually failed to follow, in a sense, in his father's boot-steps may have forced him to another arena of competition—women.

Whatever psychological stunts were diving off cliffs in Burt's brain, his relationship with Dinah caused more talk and more publicity than any relationship in Hollywood since the days when Clark Gable made a habit of marrying women decades older than he was. (His first venture down the aisle was when he was only twenty-three, with Josephine Dillon, eleven years his senior. He outdid himself six years later by marching down the aisle with Ria Langham, a wealthy forty-seven-year-old divorcée.) And much of the front page publicity could be laid directly at the feet of Burt and Dinah, who never failed to accommodate the press, always coming up with the quotable line.

Burt: "There isn't a man in California with any brains who wouldn't give his right arm to be where I am with Dinah. . . ."

Dinah: "He has a cautious, very protective attitude toward our relationship."

Burt, on younger women: "What can you do with a great pair of breasts after three or four hours?"

Dinah's friends warned her that she ought to be careful, that Burt might be using her to get some much-needed publicity to boost his sagging career. After all, she was by far the more famous of the two when they began dating. Burt was treading water in TV movies. Before Dinah, he'd been just another actor what's-his-name. Once they'd become an item, he was Burt Reynolds, symbolic savior of middle-aged women everywhere! Nonsense, Dinah assured her friends, Burt wasn't using her. She was, as she put it, "in love!" Burt also declared his feelings for the world to know. He'd fallen "in like!"

As their relationship blossomed, so did Burt's popularity on the talk-show circuit. He became a full-fledged member of the couch club, going on all the shows, Merv, Dinah, Phil, Mike, and finally, the big one, "The Tonight Show," starring the silver-haired prince, Johnny Carson.

Burt and Johnny hit it off immediately. By the time he walked out on "The Tonight Show" stage and ambled over to Johnny, his self-effacing good-ol'-boy-jus'-havin'-fun persona was finely tuned. Burt was easy pickins for Johnny, no stranger himself to the hey-I'm-just-a-small-town-boy image he'd so carefully nurtured over the years. One night they might talk about women, or all those crazy movies Burt made, or the lunatic stunts he'd performed in the early days, or Burt's new Hollywood house, up there in the hills, all decked out in red carpet and matching flocked wallpaper, five foot high wooden four-poster bed, those famous mirrors, and the huge

iron gate surrounding the whole place sporting a
gigantic "R" by the front entrance. During one
commercial break, Johnny leaned over and asked
Burt if he'd like to host "The Tonight Show"
sometime. Sure, Burt said, sure, he'd love to.

Not too long after, while in Hollywood, Burt
received a call from Johnny's people in New
York (from where "The Tonight Show" still
emanated before it eventually moved per-
manently to Burbank). His time had come. Did
he have any ideas about guests, anyone special
he'd like to have on? Yes, as a matter of fact
there was someone. A woman. A very special
woman.

eleven

A VERY special woman by the name of Judy Carne. Even though Burt and Dinah were the talk of the town, Burt chose Judy to be his first guest. They hadn't spoken a word to each other in the nearly six years since the divorce, during which time Burt's career had for the most part floundered while Judy's, in one of those cheeky art-follows-life ironies, had exploded as the sock-it-to-me girl of NBC's "Laugh-in."

Burt had "The Tonight Show" staff get in touch with Judy to invite her to be on the show. "Do you know who you're talking to?" Judy asked the voice on the other end of the line. Yes, yes, she was assured, Burt had specifically requested her and hoped she would accept the offer.

Judy arrived for the taping and was ushered to the Green Room, the place where guests wait before being introduced. She still hadn't seen Burt, who didn't want to meet with her until she made her entrance during the actual show. The moment came. Burt, seeming flustered and excited, introduced her. The audience applauded, Judy stepped out from behind the curtain, laughed and waved to the audience, walked over to a waiting Burt, kissed him lightly on the cheek, and sat down. "It was," recalled Judy, "like an acid rush!"

"How the hell are you?" she began.

"How the hell are you?" Burt replied, the pauses between each sentence were filled with laughter from the audience which was privileged, along with the rest of America, to watch the strangest reunion in the history of television take place right before their eyes.

"God, you look good," Judy said to him.

"I'm sorry to say, so do you," Burt replied. The audience loved it.

"What have you been doing?" she continued, interviewing Burt as much as he was interviewing her.

"Oh, just sitting home with my Burt and Judy towels." He then turned to the audience. "Anybody want any?" Judy added that Burt had been a monogram freak, having everything initialed BR. Shirts, spoons, "Burt's Brew" on his teacup.

Then, Burt tossed a curve. "Going with anybody?"

"Yes," Judy responded, proceeding to relate to Burt the details of her recent marriage, which had taken place in Central Park.

"A younger guy?" Burt asked, pretending to be pained by all the details.

"Yes, Burt, you know me. I hear you've gone older." It was a good come-back. Too good. The temperature in the studio dropped ten degrees. Dinah was untouchable, a heroine; Judy the ex. It was clear to Burt that Judy had overstepped the delicate boundaries of taste. He skillfully

brought her back by assuring her that, in spite of
what she said, the audience still loved her. He
even asked the audience if they did. Their applause confirmed she was going to be allowed to
live.

The show was a smash. Burt's idea to have
Judy on with him proved to be a ratings coup.
Afterward, he and Judy had a drink at Sardi's
and talked. "Burt made sure we weren't going to
be alone," Judy remembers. "The chemistry was
so much, we were both afraid. Everyone went
along to Sardi's." They embraced one final time,
then Burt took off to meet Dinah.

The show was captivating, the talk of Hollywood and New York. One person, in particular,
who'd seen it was John Boorman, the director,
then looking for an actor to play the role of
Lewis, in DELIVERANCE, James Dickey's
apocalyptic novel of the South Boorman was
about to make into a major motion picture. In
an interview, Boorman explained how he chose
Burt for the role. "I cast him right off the Carson
Show, impressed by the man's power, vulner-
ability, and style," all qualities Burt demon-
strated that night with Judy. Ironically, having
been out of movies for nearly two years, Burt
was suddenly cast in a role that had been one
of the most sought-after in Hollywood. DELIV-
ERANCE was the "big" picture, the elusive
breakthrough movie he'd been searching for.
He'd tried everything before and failed. It took
an appearance on "The Tonight Show" to do it
for him. "DELIVERANCE," Burt says, "was my

deliverance out of shit." It was the first script
he'd been offered of any quality which, he
claimed, didn't have Steve McQueen's or Robert
Redford's fingerprints on them.

If Burt was uncomfortable playing Lewis
Medlock in DELIVERANCE, his nervousness
added a positive edge to his performance. His
previous movies were built around caricatures,
Indian or detective stereotypes, or "laid-back"
tough guys who always got the girl. In DE-
LIVERANCE, there was no girl, and no badges
or headdresses, just a hard line of violence holding together a strange homophobic passion play
of sorts. DELIVERANCE was James Dickey's
Sunday School sermon; "Praise the Lord and
pass the ammunition" pragmatism, southern
style. Four men go up river on a fishing expedi-
tion, become brutalized first by the elements,
then by backwoods primitives, and finally, by
their own guilt at having survived a horrible
male-rape hunt-and-kill nightmare by resorting
to violence even more savage than what
prompted their retaliation in the first place. Doing it, Dickey suggests, is bad enough; surviving
it to live with the guilt even worse. Except for
one bow-and-arrow bit of heroism, Burt's Medlock was markedly different from anything he'd
done before. Dressed in black leather sleeveless
wet suit, Medlock was quiet, moody, tough, but
heroic rather than merely brutal. Behind the violence Burt revealed a gentleness, an assuredness
beyond the Burt in a bar with chicks and seven-
and-sevens.

DELIVERANCE also gave Burt a chance to show off his physical prowess as part of an integrated, complex, emotional performance. Much of the physical action in DELIVERANCE was dangerous and stunt people were used. Burt did convince Boorman, on one occasion, to let him try one stunt himself, and it nearly cost him his life.

One scene in DELIVERANCE called for Medlock to go over a waterfall on the Chattooga River. The film was shot on location, the waterfall was real. A specialist was called in for the shot, a "white water man." He took one look at the falls and told Boorman he was crazy, anyone going over that falls was committing suicide. He suggested Boorman use a dummy, dressed in Burt's clothes, and let it go at that. Boorman had a dummy thrown over the waterfall and that night checked it out in the rushes. "It looks like a dummy going over a waterfall," Boorman said, disgusted. Burt, also on hand to see how the shot looked told Boorman he would do the scene himself.

The next day, the scene was set, the cameras rolled, and Burt went over the falls. He was brutalized by the currents, pulled under the water and towed nearly a mile before being able to break away from the powerful tide. He was barely conscious when he reached the shore, collapsing into the hands of the crew waiting for him. "How did that look?" he asked still out of breath, badly bruised and halfway to death.

"Like a dummy going over a waterfall," Boorman said, somewhat disappointed.

"This really happened," Dickey added, reminding Burt he was acting in a "true story."

The advance word on DELIVERANCE, completed early in 1972, was sensational. It seemed a sure thing in terms of box-office, could even win a couple of oscars. There was no doubt in Burt's mind that the film would make him the superstar he wanted so much to be. Waiting for the film's release was fun-time. And what could be more fun for a good ol' boy like Burt than taking his clothes off and posing in the nude for a leading woman's magazine?

twelve

ALTHOUGH it is popularly believed that Helen Gurley Brown first suggested Burt pose in the nude for *Cosmopolitan* while both she and Burt were guesting on "The Tonight Show," that isn't quite the way it happened. By the time Brown and Burt were discussing the possibility on Johnny's show, the photo session had already taken place, the final picture selected, and the April, 1972 issue slated for its publication.

"You know why I really posed for *Cosmopolitan*? I thought it would be a kick," Burt told an interviewer. Originally, Brown had wanted another actor, but when the photos came to her desk from that session, she decided something was missing. She continued her search for the right person to be the first nude for the magazine she had recently taken over. Lots of actors and celebrities were approached. Most, including Steve McQueen, Joe Namath, and Clint Eastwood, turned her down right away, others thought it over before saying no. Stretches of the imagination included Brown's soliciting Jackie Cooper, a decidedly non-leading man type, best known as the junior half of the origi-

nal boxer-kid weeper, THE CHAMPION, made
in the thirties; even then Cooper wasn't all that
cute. "I'm not that liberated," was his way of
saying no. One famous actor did agree, but his
pictures came out so poorly Brown had to turn
him down. Desperate, Brown personally invited
Burt up to *Cosmo*'s offices. Burt, thinking he was
going to be interviewed, was a little more than
surprised when Brown made her offer. Saying
things to him like, gee, you're so *heterosexual*,
she actually got him to think it over. It would
have to be fun, he told her. It would be a ball,
she promised. He'd have to pick the picture.
Done, she said. He'd have to talk it over with
Dinah. Good enough, Brown agreed.

Big "D", as Burt liked to call Dinah, was
against the idea. She'd been on a clean-up campaign with Burt almost from the start, turning
him on to a mature weaving of two lifestyles
rather than one's being imposed on the other.
For example, she insisted they live apart. To accommodate her, Burt built a tennis court in
Jupiter. In return, Dinah added a room on to her
place for him. Even though Dinah thought the
Cosmo idea would hurt him, she agreed to
reserve final judgment until after the photo
session. Fair enough.

The photographer Brown chose for the session
was the internationally respected Francesco
Scavullo. Scavullo kept the studio unusually
cold, so cold that Burt, wearing nothing but his
toupee felt about as sexy as a lima bean. A St.
Bernard dog was added for atmosphere, along

with a bearskin rug. When Burt got the proofs, he showed them to Dinah, who changed her mind and agreed that if handled correctly, the whole thing might prove to be in good taste after all. By the time Burt and Helen Gurley Brown just happened to be on Johnny's panel, and Burt just happened to agree with Helen that his macho image was so much loose jello, and Johnny just happened to suggest that Burt ought to pose in the nude for *Cosmo*, and Burt spontaneously agreed, the April issue was all ready to go to press!

If Burt thought *Cosmo* was a joke, the industry was not amused. For all of Hollywood's libertine image, a strict code of ethics still existed. Actors, serious actors that is, didn't exceed the restrictive bounds of "good taste." To make matters worse, DELIVERANCE had gotten bogged down in post-production causing a delay in its release. Originally scheduled for late 1971, it didn't reach the screen until June, 1972, four months after the centerfold hit the stands. Having the centerfold come out before the movie did two things. First, it amplified Burt's image as a glorified personality, making him the butt of nearly a dozen jokes at the Academy Awards ceremony. Burt had become the talk of the town, all right, but the talk was mostly negative. It got so bad that everywhere he went, all anyone wanted to talk about was the centerfold. One night, having a bite to eat in a restaurant, one of the lounge musicians cracked that the only reason Burt was a big star was because of the *Cosmo* layout. Burt, not missing a beat, snapped back that the musician ought to try it, it might get him into Carnegie Hall.

Second, the centerfold created a mini-industry. Bootleg copies of the centerfold began appearing, blown up to poster-size, in stores around the country. A staggering total of two and a half *million* of these were sold as fast as they became available. The magazine itself became a collector's item; completely sold-out in two days. Brown received a memo from the Hearst circulation department complaining that people had gone to the newsstands with razor blades, and cut the centerfold out. Calls flooded the office with offers to legally merchandise the photo for jig saw puzzles, bed sheets, anything you could think of.

All of which Burt refused. He couldn't get over all the fuss caused by the photo he referred to as "the one that made me look like I'd been studying humility with Gene Barry." To his eyes, the photo was, if anything, overly modest. There was a rumor of pubic hair behind a carefully draped arm. The stiffest thing on view was a cigar, the smile on Burt's face as pure as a new-born baby's. At first he made jokes about the guy who'd been rejected before him by Brown. "He's probably seeing his analyst every day." The illegal posters, though, were no laughing matter. He threatened to sue, but who? By the time one manufacturer could be tracked down, five more would just as easily take his place.

By May, the initial storm had begun to quiet

down. Almost as if to atone for the uproar and just weeks before the scheduled release, finally, of DELIVERANCE, Burt offered to personally autograph a copy of the centerfold and personally deliver it to the highest bidder for the FIGHT FOR SIGHT campaign, one of the many charitable organizations he was becoming involved with, and would continue to be involved with in the future. However, when DELIVERANCE was released, nearly every review referred as much to *Cosmo* as to Medlock. There was no question in Burt's mind, and in everyone else's, that when the Academy Award nominations were announced for the following year, and Burt's name was left out for best actor, it was not because of his performance, but because of his centerfold. It was enough to drive a man up a tree. Or at least a tree house.

thirteen

IT seemed everywhere he looked, he saw that centerfold, or an article in a newspaper or magazine about it. To make matters worse, United Artists quick-released FUZZ, a film he'd made with his old "pal" Raquel Welch, one of those Burt-plays-detective action flicks, now overlapping DELIVERANCE. And there was a third picture in release, Woody Allen's EVERYTHING YOU WANTED TO KNOW ABOUT SEX BUT WERE AFRAID TO ASK. As a favor to Allen, Burt played the macho leader of a team of sperm about to be "launched". To Burt it was just a joke, a change of pace. If nobody seemed to be laughing, it was because the timing of everything had been thrown completely off by Burt's appearance in *Cosmo*. The month following the centerfold, Burt hastily signed to play the lead in THE RAINMAKER at the Toledo Music Theatre for one week, for $30,000. Although the show was a financial smash, every seat, every standing place sold out, and Burt's salary established a new record for summer and winter stock; his performance—the one aspect was really interested in—was completely overshadowed by his notoriety. There was no question that the record-breaking grosses were a result of Burt's nude layout.

Movies, centerfolds, cameos, interviews, posters. It all seemed, to Burt, a crazy quilt of bad timing. Every serious attempt at acting he made, like THE RAINMAKER or DELIVERANCE, was offset by an overkill of Reynoldsmania that reached its peak when the Lion County Safari Club of Los Angeles nominated Burt as the "Sensuous Man Of The Year." He was even invited to judge the Miss Nude Universe contest.

Even sniffy Beverly Hills, with its above-it-all attitude couldn't resist teasing Burt. After an article ran in the L.A. papers about how the Motion Picture Academy's legendary library and archive was having trouble keeping its copies of the notorious *Cosmo* April issue from being stolen, the famous GIORGIO'S of Beverly Hills, one of the most exclusive boutiques in the world, built its Rodeo Drive window around a copy of the centerfold. No sooner did it go on display than offers came pouring into the shop from people desperate to get their hands on a copy. When anyone bothered to ask Burt about all the attention he was getting, he angrily rejected the idea that the centerfold had made him a celebrity. He'd been a celebrity for years, damnit! No, Burt insisted, the centerfold hadn't made him; he'd made the centerfold, and along with it the new image of *Cosmopolitan*.

Although Burt was now deluged with movie offers, he turned most of them down because they either contained a nude scene (for him, not

his co-star) or they were silly exploitation movies
with little for him to do besides look sexy
and wear skimpy costumes. Instead, he opted
for SHAMUS, a Columbia Pictures detective
yarn with Burt back in familiar territory, playing the hard-nosed detective who gets the girl.
SHAMUS was shot on location in New York, in
the very same neighborhood where, just a few
years earlier, Burt had been completely anonymous filming "Hawk." Now, hordes of screaming
women followed him everywhere, tearing impa-
tiently at his clothes, requiring the studio to hire
bodyguards to protect him. The local newspapers
were filled with stories about women trying to
break into Burt's hotel room. Inevitably, the
gossips began to run stories linking Burt and his
co-star, Dyan Cannon, stories which were ignored
by Burt and Dyan, and by Dinah, three thousand miles away, busy at work on her own
daytime TV show.

During the filming of SHAMUS, Burt was
forbidden to do any stunt work. Hal Needham
wasn't available, and there was one jump Burt
really wanted to make. It took an awful lot of
convincing, but the producers finally got him to
agree to let a stuntman do it. Everyone watched
as the guy leapt into the air—and completely
missed his target, falling twenty-five feet to the
ground, breaking most of his ribs, lingering near
death for several days. Burt blamed the producers for the accident. Had they allowed him to
do the stunt, he told them, he would have been
able to pull it off with no sweat.

There were those that felt Burt was trying

harder than ever to establish, perhaps re-establish his macho image after *Cosmo*. He even began to quote Hemingway to friends, "The closer to death you are, the more precious life becomes." It may have made good copy, but it didn't sit that well with Dinah, who was privately telling friends she was afraid one day he'd kill himself doing those foolish stunts he was so crazy about.

As soon as SHAMUS was finished, the producers rush-released it into theatres, correctly anticipating that anything with Burt's name on it meant big box-office. Meanwhile, Burt, anxious to take a break from Hollywood, called Big D and told her he was coming to pick her up and take her to Jupiter.

The transformation at the ranch was simply amazing. Burt, Sr. had worked the weary, swampy land into a plush, fertile grazing pasture, complete with Angus steer dotting the acreage in all directions as far as the eye could see. The main house, where Burt's parents lived, was the picture of rustic modernism—wagon wheels and wooden tabletops, wood paneling and high ceiling beams, and what Burt referred to as the largest collection of "insignificant oils in Florida." Above the front entrance to the house were the two .45's that Burt had used during his "Gunsmoke" days, a sharp reminder of where it had all come from.

Behind the main house was a smaller, more private one for Burt. The focus of this cottage was the framed photograph of Burt in bed with

Angie Dickenson, in a scene from the 1969
SAM WHISKEY, hanging directly over the
four-poster. Under the photo, in large lettering,
was the caption, "An actor's life is hell." The
place also sported a sunken bath, a steam room,
and a gym stocked with every conceivable piece
of weight-lifting equipment (which Burt swore
he never touched). The house was decked out, of
course, in Burt's favorite color combo, bordello
red and black.

His real source of pride, though, was his own
personal stairway to heaven a mile west of the
main house. Atop a particularly thick and rugged
tree sat Burt's private dream, a custom-made,
luxurious tree house. The circular staircase which
led up to the entrance was supported by a brick
foundation, which also held up the heavy,
wooden front door. The whole exterior, including
the bricks, had been painted in camouflage
brown and greens, making the tree house all but
invisible from as near as fifty yards. Inside, the
camouflage scheme was continued. Besides a
fully functioning kitchen, a master bedroom and
a Japanese-style bath, there was a stereo system
with nine separate sets of speakers, and lush
green bark-to-bark carpeting to the tune of $8,-
000. Through the rear entrance and over a
swinging bridge was a gazebo with a view of the
two lakes which ran alongside, artificially raised
and well stocked with bass. Burt loved to sit
back on a chair and feed ice-cubes to his friendly
alligator, Fred, who lived in the little "moat"
surrounding the tree house. Burt would ride,
with Dinah, on horseback across his 180-acre

spread, galloping as far away from the *Cosmo* craziness as his horse could take him, trying to forget the pandemonium that had plagued him since the centerfold had become the centerpiece of his career.

Down in Jupiter, his biggest problem was what to do with the branding irons he'd bought. "I don't know how to brand anything," Burt confessed, as he and Burt, Sr. contemplated the future of the ranch. Dismayed by the lack of steer production—"I've got the only homosexual bulls in the country"—Burt began to play with the idea of maybe raising horses; Appaloosas. As Burt and Dinah left the ranch, the sign hanging over the entrance was already being changed to read, THE BURT REYNOLDS HORSE RANCH, OWNED BY BURT REYNOLDS SENIOR AND BURT REYNOLDS JUNIOR.

He knew he was back in Hollywood when a drunk in an elevator asked if he'd sign his belly-button. "How about me signing your mouth?" Burt replied. Exasperated, he told one reporter, "When I list the three most unimportant events in my life, *Cosmo* will be one of them." As if to demonstrate that his career was making movies, not excuses, he plunged into yet another movie.

An action-adventure yarn, WHITE LIGHT-NING was familiar territory to Burt. As Gator McKlusky, he was out to avenge the death of his kid brother at the hands of some evil city officials. It felt good to be back on a set again, with the familiar, reliable pros chuckling at the inside gags, the grips and the gaffers sipping hot coffee

out of containers, the actors quietly going over
their lines while another stunt was being set.
Burt was relieved to have Needham back, his
premier stuntman and best pal once again available for work on Burt's projects after fulfilling
numerous other commitments. Throughout all
the *Cosmo* turmoil, it had been Needham who'd
stood by Burt, who'd urged his buddy to keep
making movies, their kind of movies, lots of action, lots of stunts, to turn a deaf ear to the
bad-mouth gossip Needham felt Burt didn't
deserve. Now, in WHITE LIGHTNING, the
script called for the type of stunts Burt and
Needham specialized in, the life-risking cliff-
hangers.

Burt and Hal Needham took their movie work
seriously. For all the bravado they shared off-
screen, they both understood that stunt work
was no-nonsense time, requiring pinpoint preci-
sion and timing. On the set, Burt's concentration
was total, as if his life, or Hal's, depended upon
it—which it often did.

In Little Rock, at five in the afternoon on
the bank of the Arkansas River, Burt stared
hard at the next set-up, never breaking his
concentration for a second. This one was dangerous, a "one-timer," no second chances. A car,
driven by Gator (Burt), flies off a highway and
lands on a floating barge, seemingly suspended in
space for five agonizing seconds. Needham, ice in
his aluminum veins, signaled from inside the
specially prepped Ford he was ready. Taking a
deep breath, he gunned her for all she was worth.
Inches from the edge of the road, he suddenly

slammed on the brakes, clouding out in a burst
of sand. Everyone held his breath until Needham emerged, finally, from the car, waving with
his arms to signal he was all right. "Not enough
speed," he said to Burt, as the crew set up the
re-take.

Once again it was go time. Revving up the engine, Needham yanked his foot off the clutch and
sent the car flying; this time not holding back
when it shot off the road in a mockery of
madness. The Ford came pounding down, crash-
ing onto the lip of the barge, almost, but not
quite teeter-tottering smack into the river. The
front-end was all that was keeping the Ford, and
Needham, on the barge. Seconds passed, and
there was no sign from inside the car. "Get a
doctor," someone screamed, as the car started to
slip into the river. Suddenly, the hundred-plus
crew burst into motion, everyone seeming to run
in a different direction at the same time. Burt
dove into the water, swam to the Ford, and
dragged Needham's groggy body out the front
window. Outstretched hands waited for them at
the edge of the river, pulling Burt and Needham
to safety. Admist the burst of applause from the
crew, Burt, dripping wet, quietly suggested to
the film's producers that the sequence could be
used if the scene was rewritten.

WHITE LIGHTNING finished shooting as
1972 came to an end. It had been quite a year
for Burt. DELIVERANCE was a box-office
smash, as was SHAMUS, the two films combining to put Burt on the Top Ten Box Office Star

list for the first time; at number four, behind his pals Clint Eastwood and Ryan O'Neal, numbers one and two, and Steve McQueen, number three. Behind Burt were Robert Redford, Barbra Streisand, Paul Newman, Charles Bronson, John Wayne, and, lingering back at number ten, none other than Marlon Brando. The year had, indeed, been a twelve-month stretch filled with incredible highs, as well as depressing lows. If 1972 had its share of bad dreams, though, 1973 would prove to be one gigantic nightmare.

fourteen

THE rumors began after Christmas, 1972, almost as soon as Burt and Dinah left Jupiter. A local Florida radio station broke into its regularly scheduled program to break the news that Burt and Dinah were going to make it official; they'd taken out a wedding license and were getting married on the ranch. The news was picked up by the wire services and within minutes the ranch was being beseiged by phone calls from journalists all over the country hungry for the details. Burt, Sr. became so annoyed at the constant ringing of the phone he simply took it off the hook for the rest of the night.

At the very moment Burt and Dinah were supposedly tying the knot in Jupiter, they were actually in Arizona, where Burt was announcing his intention to chair the 1973 Easter Seals Telethon. They were in Gila Bend, Arizona because the dusty, leftover village was the location of his next movie, about to go into production. THE MAN WHO LOVED CAT DANCING, co-starring Sarah Miles, was the second "big" picture of his career.

In CAT DANCING, a one-time army officer

turned outlaw falls in love with a high-spirited
Indian squaw, Cat Dancing. By "taming" her
savage behavior, he manages to liberate her, socially and sexually. It was all there, the Indian/
woman overtones, the aggressive heroics, and, for
a change, the big budget. Never mind that the
dialogue Burt would be required to act would
contain lines like these, in response to a question
from Cat Dancing about why people fall in love:
"I dunno. I suppose it's like two drops of rain
that fall together and become one." Jim Aubrey,
the head of MGM, who'd personally courted
Burt for the role, told him to forget the dialogue
and forget the plot. It's the chemistry the audience will go nuts over, Aubrey insisted, the
chemistry between Burt Reynolds and Sarah
Miles.

CAT DANCING was Aubrey's baby from the
start. Having been summarily fired as the head
of programming for CBS by William Paley over
"creative differences," i.e. low ratings, Aubrey
eventually took over the reins at MGM, his goal
being to lift the faltering studio out of its financial doldrums, caused in part by its steadfast refusal to get into TV production, resulting in an
abundance of unused studio space, and steadily
declining revenues. Aubrey's plan, after settling
in at the legendary Culver City studio, was to
concentrate on the "big" picture, to revive
MGM's slightly tarnished image as the studio of
opulence. The first project he earmarked for the
big push was CAT DANCING.

There was no question in Aubrey's mind who
to cast in the male lead. Burt Reynolds' name

Fern and Burt Reynolds, Sr.

Burt behind the wheel

The wedding

The reception

Burt and Judy in the Hollywood Hills, 1964

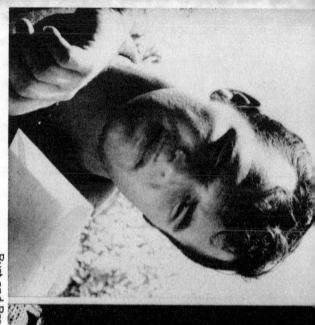

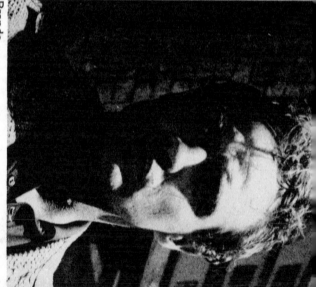

Burt and Brando
Inspiration or nemesis

Lori Nelson, Burt's one-time fiancée, Burt, and Darren
McGavin, relaxing on the set of *Riverboat*

The Early Years on TV:

Burt as Hawk

Burt with Johnny

The Man Who Loved Cat Dancing

Burt arriving for the inquest

Sarah arriving for the inquest

Burt, Sarah outside the courthouse

Burt at his home in Jupiter

Jill Clayburgh

Leading Ladies:

Dyan Cannon

Lesley-Anne Down

Lauren Hutton

Sally Field

Rachel Ward

The Longest Yard

Semi-Tough

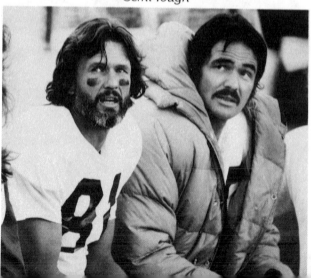

Along the Hollywood Walk of Fame...
and Sunset Boulevard

Sky-high in *Hooper*

With Needham

With
Barbara
Walters

With Fonda and Beatty

Burt and Dinah on the air

Burt with Big D.

With Sally

With Tawny

BURT REYNOLDS

ASK ME WHAT I AM

On the record

Calling the shots

was on everybody's lips. Aubrey probably didn't mind at all that much of Reynolds' publicity was due to his having posed in the nude for *Cosmopolitan*. He understood bottom line. That's why he was the head of MGM. Aubrey courted Burt royally, pointing out along the way that CAT DANCING was going first class, all the way. Eleanor Perry, the prestigious producer-writer of DAVID AND LISA fame was going to co-produce, with Martin Poll, and write the script. Richard Sarafian was earmarked to direct. While having virtually no film experience, Aubrey convinced Burt that Sarafian would pose no "problems", being a good, workman-like director. Aubrey might have added, if he'd been so inclined, that Sarafian was a veteran of numerous television shows made under Aubrey's personal supervision, leaving little doubt it would be Aubrey, himself, calling most of the CAT DANCING shots. Rounding out an impressive supporting cast was Lee J. Cobb, legendary fifties film and stage actor. And, topping off the whole package, Aubrey threw in Jay Silverheels, TV's Tonto, to play an Indian, a gesture no doubt meant to appeal to Burt's sensitivity toward the burgeoning Indian militancy just beginning to rear its head in Hollywood—a movement organized and led by Marlon Brando.

As convincing as Aubrey was, right down to his MGM-Hires-Indian-posturing, CAT DANCING wasn't Burt's first choice of the next "big" movie he wanted to make. Somewhere along the way he'd picked up a copy of Dan Jenkins' football novel, SEMI-TOUGH, a hip profile of jock life, on the field and in the bedroom. Having approached Jenkins about the possibility of acquiring his novel, Burt discovered that he was too late, the rights had been snatched up by David Merrick. When Burt called Merrick to tell him he could stop searching for an actor to play Billy Clyde Puckett, that he, Burt, *was* Billy Clyde, Merrick said fine, fine, but there was just one hitch. SEMI-TOUGH was going to be a Broadway musical.

With SEMI-TOUGH out of the picture, Burt accepted CAT DANCING. It's worth noting that a short time later, Burt decided to cut an album if for no other reason than to prove to David Merrick he could carry a tune. Hiring Bobby Goldsboro, a former teen idol turned record producer, Burt recorded "Ask Me What I Am," on Mercury Records. It did fairly well, with Burt's fans rushing to hear his interpretation of such classics as "Childhood 1949," "The First One That I Lay With," "You Can't Always Sing a Happy Song," and of course, everybody's favorite, "There's a Slight Misunderstanding Between God And Man." Although anything with Burt's photo on it would do well, the critical reception was something else again. From the Chicago Tribune, Burt received one of the kinder reviews: "He's a would-be singer, since his voice leans as much toward heavy breathing as baritone and manages to be as mediocre as most of his material . . . and "I Like Having You Around" features Reynolds' chum, Dinah Shore in the background valiantly carrying on her continual struggle to stay on key."

"I don't know," Goldsboro commented, when asked his opinion of the album, "Burt has a nice voice." As for Dinah's take on Burt's singing, while always encouraging, Burt did notice that whenever they were driving somewhere and Dinah would start to sing, she would always stop when he'd begin to harmonize with her; sometimes flicking on the radio, other times continuing the ride in silence. No one knows for sure if Merrick ever actually heard the album or not, but Burt was never in the running for the musical version of SEMI-TOUGH.

Burt's co-star in CAT DANCING, Sarah Miles, was a veteran of the rumor mills on both sides of the Atlantic. Married to movie director and a screenwriter, Robert Bolt, of A MAN FOR ALL SEASONS fame, she'd been linked romantically with many of England's and Hollywood's biggest names. Rumors that her marriage was in trouble surfaced again when she announced that she'd be coming to America to do CAT DANCING, while Bolt would remain in England. While starring in one rumor after another, American audiences had actually seen her in only one major feature, Harold Pinter's THE SERVANT, a bizarre movie which featured the nubile Miles in an unforgettable shirt-lifting seduction scene that caused male veiwers to sweat long after Pinter's script had ceased to make them think. Obviously, Aubrey was calculating box-office dynamite pairing Reynolds and Miles in a screenplay loaded to the spurs with sexual innuendo. CAT DANCING, as Aubrey saw it, would be a visual feast of day-old growth, husky voice and broad shoulders lap-dissolving with sexy legs, bare feet, haughty breasts, shiny wet black hair and moist lips. So complete was Aubrey's campaign to turn CAT DANCING into an "event," the highest form of "big" movie, he invited the indefatigable Merv Griffen to visit the location site, Gila Bend, to shoot a segment around Burt as part of a TV "Special" Merv was doing which happened to coincide with the scheduled release date of CAT DANCING: Christmas, 1973.

Filming began early in February. Burt, as always, preferred to travel alone when he worked, excluding even Dinah from staying with him on location. Sarah Miles, however, brought a personal coterie with her, including a governess, Jane Evans, to care for her five-year-old son, and David A. Whiting, Miles' "personal assistant." Whiting had lived with Miles and Bolt in their English mansion and was now to share the actress' suite on location, to care for her everyday needs. Whiting was part accountant, part secretary, and part gofer (go for this, go for that . . .).

Almost from the start, there was friction on the set between Burt and Whiting. Unfortunately, Whiting saw himself as "indispensable" to Miles, his way of dealing with the fact that he had fallen in love with his vivacious employer. To put it bluntly, Whiting was a Sarah Miles groupie, or would-be groupie as there is no evidence of any sexual relationship between the two other than the one in Whiting's fantasies. Whiting expressed his one-sided affection for Miles through his obsessive attention to detail, doting on her every whim, taking it upon himself to "protect" her from any annoyances, his perverse rationale for isolating her, to keep her all to himself. Even if Burt hadn't become immediately friendly with his co-star, which he did; even if he hadn't been a little flirtatious, which he was, his very presence became a furious threat to Whiting's delicate balance, causing the young man to increase his daily intake of quaaludes.

The first time Sarah Miles noticed anything peculiar in Whiting's behavior on location was when he began slipping back into his "moods," depressions he'd suffered while in England which produced a lethargic, hazy attitude quite apart from his normally meticulous demeanor. When he was in one of his moods, he'd always want to talk with Miles; talks which would turn to gloomy monologues on the subject of creativity, or Whiting's lack of it.

Once shooting began, Whiting had to be told continually to please keep off the set, that the set was only for those directly connected with the movie, that his presence was not welcome while shooting was in progress. Wanting to avoid any possible confrontations between Burt and Whiting, Miles tried to keep her "secretary" as busy as possible. Nevertheless, after the first week's shooting, late Friday afternoon, February 9th, when Miles had finally gotten the last of the red-tint make-up off her body, she noticed that Whiting was once again slipping into one of his

moods. Even though she was exhausted from the
day's work, and Merv Griffen and crew were arriving on the set early Saturday morning, Miles
asked Whiting to have a couple of drinks with
her, in order to try and cheer him up. They went
to the motel lounge where Sarah was immediately recognized by a couple of extras, local
wranglers hired by Sarafian to add some color to
the film. Excited by the prospect of chatting up
some real cowboys, Sarah graciously accepted
their invitation to join them. Soon, they were all
laughing and drinking and having a pretty good
time.

Except Whiting, who was becoming incensed
with Sarah; how dare she go slumming like this,
when she was supposed to be working hard at
cheering him up! Outraged, Whiting insisted she
leave with him immediately and return to the
suite. Reluctantly, perhaps not wanting to upset
Whiting any further, Miles left with him.

The next morning, February 10th, Merv arrived on schedule, and proceeded to completely
disrupt Sarafian's shooting day, causing re-take
after re-take, exhausting cast and crew alike in a
day Aubrey willingly sacrificed for promotion.
Merv, thrilled with how things were going, decided to throw a bash for the whole gang. Ar-
rangements were made at the Pink Palomino,
some forty miles from Gila Bend. Word came
down from Aubrey himself that everyone was to
attend, including Reynolds and Miles. Whiting,
though, was excluded by Miles, who told him the
party was only for those working directly on the

picture. Burt asked Miles if she'd like to go with him to the party and she agreed. Neither was anxious to attend; they'd make an obligatory appearance, then head back to the motel.

At the party, Burt, smiling and pleasant, had a drink with Merv and talked over the possibility of Merv producing a series of TV specials for him. Miles, though, was completely turned off to the whole affair. She couldn't understand why Americans always ate so much food. The film had so far been one long buffet constantly gobbled up by overweight crew members, now once again stuffing their faces with every conceivable type of cold-cut known to mankind, wedged between the thickest, dryest bread she'd ever seen. After only a few minutes, she decided she'd had enough and was ready to leave. Lee J. Cobb, also bored by the party, didn't mind at all when Miles asked him if she could ride back with him. Saying her good-byes, she got into Lee J. Cobb's car and let the burly actor drive her back to the motel. Burt left shortly after.

Merv's party didn't break up until well after 1:00 A.M. Sunday morning. The various cast and crew members piled into cars and began the forty-mile caravan back to Gila Bend. Everyone had turned out for Merv's bash and was eager to hit the sack before the next day's shooting. Even though it was Sunday, there was a full day's work ahead. However, this Sunday would be unlike anything planned or expected by the CAT DANCING organization. For, at a little past 11:00 that morning, Sarah Miles entered her Travel Lodge motel suite bathroom and discov-

ered the body of David A. Whiting, sprawled
across the tile floor, ice-cold dead.

Headlines screamed across the country. They
stretched all the way to London with the news of
Whiting's death. Several days passed before the
coroner was able to furnish official cause, an overdose of quaaludes. Even before this belated an-
nouncement was made, the public was being
reassured by the sensationalistic press that there
was more there than met the eye. There were
rumors of an ongoing affair between Burt and
Sarah Miles. Burt, Miles and Whiting were the
talk of Beverly Hills soirees. While the gossip
may have upset those involved, it didn't seem to
bother Aubrey all that much; scandal was
front-page news, and that kind of publicity you
couldn't buy for a million dollars. His glee began
to dim, though, when, out of nowhere, Whiting's
mother, Mrs. Louise Campbell, appeared on the
scene in Arizona, demanding an official inquest be
held into the death of her son. She was absolutely certain foul play had been involved, and,
she insisted, she could prove it.

HOW DID DAVID WHITING REALLY
DIE? became the latest headline out of Gila
Bend. Mrs. Campbell's attorney, John P. Frank,
former law clerk to Supreme Court Justice Hugo
L. Black and a former law professor at Yale,
made the stunning accusation that there was a
"planned cover-up of prominent persons involved in the death" of David A. Whiting. He
followed up this public statement with a signed
affidavit from Dr. Bernard B. Brodie, professor

of pharmacology at the University of Arizona, claiming the amount of drugs found in Whiting's body was not likely to cause death.

Three weeks later, an official inquest was ordered. Three subpoenas were issued; one for Sarah Miles, one for Burt Reynolds, and one for Miles' governess, Jane Evans. MGM immediately had its attorney, John J. Flynn, seek a restraining order to prevent Burt and Sarah Miles from having to personally appear, on the grounds that any delay in production might prove to be prohibitively expensive, resulting in perhaps the shelving of the entire project. Shooting had been completed in Gila Bend and was back on the MGM lot. Economics, not justice, seemed Aubrey's primary concern.

Burt was edgy, nervous at the prospect of having to return to Gila Bend. On the day he received his subpoena, Burt had lunch with Sarah Miles at the MGM lot where they were joined by Judy Carne, of all people. Later that night, Burt had dinner with Dinah Shore, while revelations continued to pour out of the Arizona investigation, details centering around the events of the night of February 10th, 1973, between the time Burt and Sarah Miles left Merv's party, separately, until the discovery of Whiting's body, some fifteen hours later. The more the public found out, the more intrigued it became. Mrs. Campbell's version of the events were quite different than Burt's and Miles'.

To reconstruct what actually took place, it's necessary to pick up the events from the party at the Pink Palomino; events not fully examined

at the inquest where Burt and Sarah Miles were
eventually forced to personally testify. The following information was obtained by examining
publicly available documents, and from confiden-
tial interviews.

On the night of February 9th, Sarah Miles
and Lee J. Cobb returned to the Travel Lodge
Motel at approximately 9:30 P.M. Sarah went
to her suite, where David Whiting was waiting
for her. Burt returned to the motel alone and
was in his room by midnight. Shortly thereafter,
Letzo Roberts, a Japanese masseuse, knocked on
Burt's door, arriving to administer a rubdown
prearranged by Burt. Roberts waited for what
seemed to be an unusually long time before Burt
opened the door. When he finally did, he was
wearing a terrycloth robe. He gestured for Letzo
to enter his room, which she did, noticing for the
first time that Burt was not alone. Sarah Miles
was also present.

"Oh, Sarah, what are you doing here?" Letzo
asked. Miles nodded as Burt answered, "Sarah is
hiding." With that, Miles reportedly watched as
Letzo instructed Burt to remove his robe and lie
on the bed. Miles sat alongside, eating first an
apple, then a banana, her eyes fixed on Letzo's
hands as they smoothly oiled Burt's back. The
massage took two hours, during which time
Sarah turned on the TV set and fell asleep. Letzo
asked Burt if he needed any help in getting
Sarah back to her suite, to which he replied,
"No, just leave her there." Letzo departed at
2:30 A.M.

According to testimony given by Sarah Miles

at the inquest, she was awakened by Burt who
returned her to her suite, at 3:15 A.M. Miles
testified that when she entered she was surprised
to find David Whiting awake and waiting for
her. "Where have you been?" she testified he demanded.

"That's none of your business, none of your
business, none of your business," Miles reportedly repeated, over and over again, disgusted
with Whiting's obsessive harping.

"If you don't tell me, I'm going to kill you,"
Whiting shouted, grabbing Miles and throwing
her against the motel room wall. Miles began
screaming, loud enough to be heard by Jane
Evans, the nurse in the next room who came
running to see what was the matter. Rushing
into Sarah Miles' suite, she saw Whiting all over
the actress and tried to pull him off. Miles
screamed for Evans to call Burt on the phone,
which Evans did. By the time he arrived, only a
few moments later, Whiting and the nurse were
both out of the suite, at least out of Burt's sight,
as he would later testify. Sarah Miles was
crumpled on her motel suite floor, a lump the
size of a jumbo egg on her head, blood pouring
from her lower lip. Burt insisted she spend the
rest of the night in his room, which she did.

The next morning, at approximately 11:00
A.M., Sarah Miles, according to her testimony,
returned to her suite and discovered Whiting's
body. She went screaming back to Burt's room,
pounding on his door until he opened it. "David
is in the room" she mumbled, dumbstruck.

*   *   *

When it was Burt's turn to testify, he was, understandably, furious. Stepping off the plane in Gila Bend, he was surrounded by reporters. He referred to presiding Judge Winsor, as "that plumber." In fact, Winsor's occupation was that of a plumber, Gila Bend not being a town normally in need of a full-time judge. Burt's feeling was that the judge was conducting "a circus," using the inquest to maybe put himself, as well as Gila Bend, on the map.

On the stand, Burt's face was tense, his brow as wrinkled as the brown suit he wore in the overheated courthouse. His testimony coincided with that of Sarah Miles'. He told the court he'd only met Whiting twice, and that he "definitely did not see him that night." In low, measured tones, Burt testified how he found Whiting's body the next morning. "Whiting was in a very strange, very awkward position, his arm bent up behind him. There was a plastic pill container in his hand. There were pills on his arm. There were pills all over the place. I don't know why I did it unless it was something I learned in the movies, but I felt for his pulse . . . there was no pulse. I took the pill container out of his hand, like a dummy." He further testified that the pill bottle had a prescription label on it, but that he didn't read it. Questioned about what could have happened to the bottle, he replied he must have lost it.

Meanwhile, the press was releasing bombshells. No one was able to pinpoint where the information was leaking from, but somebody had all but hooked a hose up to the front pages of newspapers on both sides of the Atlantic. For example, one newspaper wondered, how come Burt and Sarah Miles arrived at the party Saturday evening as a couple, but left separately? Was this done deliberately, so that the rest of the cast and crew would not realize they were maybe carrying on an affair and trying to cover tracks? Another paper inquired, based upon the testimony given, just what, or who was Sarah Miles hiding from when Letzo Roberts arrived at Burt's room for his massage?

Another bombshell went off when it was disclosed by Whiting's mother that there were unexplained bruises all over Whiting's body and a one-inch star-shaped laceration on the back of his head.

Was Whiting still in Sarah Miles' room when Burt, responding to Jane Evans' panicky phone call, arrived? No one seemed able to place Whiting anywhere between the time Burt received the phone call and the time he got to Miles' suite. If Whiting wasn't in the suite, then where the hell was he?

And no one could place Burt and Sarah Miles anywhere from the time they left Merv's party, between 8:30 and 9:30 P.M., and a little past midnight, when Letzo Roberts placed them both in Burt's room. The only statement Sarah would make on the subject was that she absolutely had had no physical contact with Burt at any time. On the stand, though, she was about to drop the biggest bombshell yet. The court wanted to know what she did after Burt discovered the body. It was established that she was pretty much out of control, hysterical perhaps. Had she returned to her room again, after Burt's? Yes. Why, the court wanted to know. "To take my birth pill." Ka-boom.

The press was convinced that not only had Burt and Sarah Miles had an affair, but the "unexplained" bruise on the back of Whiting's head was caused either by a ring worn on a finger, or a bare knuckle when somebody beat up on Whiting. However, neither Burt nor Sarah Miles were challenged on any part of their testimony. They were allowed to return to Hollywood, at which time Jim Aubrey ordered an immediate resumption of filming.

It would be another three weeks before the official inquest would end, three weeks which saw Burt's concentration dissipate to the point where a simply staged fight scene between him and Jack Warden resulted in Burt's being injured so seriously he had to be rushed to the hospital, where surgery was indicated. No, Burt insisted, he would finish the picture before having the operation.

It was, in Burt's words, "the most terrible time in my life." The only bright spot during all this was Dinah. "She really is the best female friend I have, and maybe the *best* friend," he declared, as if in response to her having flown to his side staying with him from the instant the story first hit the papers; never leaving him for a moment during the inquest; never doubting, publicly or privately, that Burt was totally innocent.

On March 22nd, the inquest ruled that

David A. Whiting, twenty-six years old, died of
an overdose of drugs, specifically methaqualone,
or quaaludes, and that the death was officially
considered a suicide. The jury, four men and two
women, released its own statement to the press
in an attempt to explain its verdict. It complained that the bruises and the star-shaped laceration had not been sufficiently explained, but
that it did not overrule the coroner's finding of
cause of death attributable to drugs. Judge Winsor, in turn, expressed his dissatisfaction with
the jury and with the whole inquest in general,
commenting to the press that there were "a lot
of unanswered things and contradictions" in the
testimony. On the heels of Winsor's statement
came one from Dr. Frederick Meyers, professor
of pharmacology at the University of California
Medical Center at San Francisco. Another of
Mrs. Campbell's "staff," Dr. Meyers concluded
that as far as he was concerned, "No cause of
death has been established." Mrs. Campbell publicly accused Arizona officials of conducting a
perfunctory investigation, and, in all fairness,
she was probably right. Regardless of anyone's
guilt or innocence, Gila Bend simply wasn't
ready, equipped, or experienced to handle a case
as volatile as this one, inevitably resulting in
what Burt had accurately described as a circus.

Even after the Police Chief of Gila Bend announced, on March 23rd, that the case was officially closed, Mrs. Campbell refused to give up.
As far as she was concerned, this was only the
beginning. She was going to have another au-
topsy performed on her son's body, at her own

expense if need be. She was going to investigate
everything. *Everything!* As if responding
directly to Mrs. Campbell, the jury hastily
called a press conference, this time to announce
the fact that they were convinced that Whiting
had indeed been in a fight before his death,
which would logically explain those bruises and
the star-shaped laceration. However, not one bit
of evidence had been presented to them suggesting anyone who might have been involved with
Whiting in that fight. It went on to criticize the
officers in charge of the investigation for having
carelessly failed questioning any other guests in
the motel the night of Whiting's death.

Barely a week after the case was closed, Burt
was rushed to the hospital for emergency surgery, resulting from his injury. By his side the
entire time was Dinah, there, as always, to hold
his hand.

Meanwhile, James Bacon, the celebrated
columnist for the Los Angeles Herald-Examiner,
ran a column defending Burt's integrity. In the
piece, Bacon quoted extensively Dave Gershenson, Burt's publicist. Ironically, Gershenson's
impassioned defense of Burt's character sounded
exactly like that—a defense. Gershenson stated
flatly that "Burt Reynolds never laid a glove on
David Whiting before the latter died of an apparent overdose of pills."

The delays caused by the inquest and Burt's
surgery, which was reported to be for a hernia but
was whispered to be for a bleeding ulcer, were
starting to add up to a lot of money. More than

$50,000 had already been lost in production costs alone. When Burt was released from the hospital, he was advised by his doctors to take it very easy; that still more surgery was indicated, as soon as filming was completed. Aubrey, meanwhile, remained adamant about finishing the film without any further delays. Needing additional outdoor footage, Aubrey changed the location site, for obvious reasons, from Gila Bend to Utah, during which time Burt and the rest of the cast and crew were exposed to flash floods, hail storms, and bitter cold. Finally, the first week in April, THE MAN WHO LOVED CAT DANCING finished shooting. Then, and only then, would Burt make any public comment on what had taken place. He complained about the press coverage, and the lack of actual interviews with himself or Sarah Miles. "They left all those gaps in the stories. When you do that, lots of people fill in the gaps with ugly thoughts." As to what Sarah was doing in Burt's room, and that gash on Whiting's head, Burt replied that, "Yes, Sarah was in my room while I was getting a massage. Massage didn't used to be a dirty word. No, I didn't want Sarah there. I asked her to leave but she wouldn't . . . If I'd found Whiting beating up Sarah, then, being the male chauvinist pig that I am, I'd have fought with him. But he wouldn't have had that so-called gash, which was just a quarter-inch cut, probably the result of a fall.

"I know the penalty for perjury. I said under oath that I did not see, touch or physically harm David Whiting that night. I would have been glad to say under oath that I did not have an affair with Sarah Miles, but nobody asked." Burt reserved his highest praise, though, for Dinah, referring to her as a "pressure ballplayer," adding, "She never doubted, never questioned. That's class. I'd be happy if I had half of Dinah's class."

Shortly after the completion of CAT DANCING, Burt Reynolds collapsed, reportedly from exhaustion, then dropped totally out of sight for eight weeks, telling nobody, except Dinah and Hal Needham, where he was. So completely did he erase himself from the public that rumors of his death began to emerge. Or that he was terminally ill. Or that he'd suffered a massive heart attack. One report speculated that he may have met with a violent end as a result of the Gila Bend incident. The one thing everyone agreed on, though, was that nobody knew where the hell he was.

fifteen

JUPITER, Florida: that's where he was. Hal
Needham had reportedly arranged to sneak Burt
away from the hospital through a side door while
the press gathered out front to converge on him.
Needham drove Burt, in a motor-home, to a private plane, where, joined by Dinah, he took off
for home. He was fed up with Hollywood. "I
don't belong in places like New York or Los Angeles," he told a friend. "I should be on a farm
with a few cases of beer," which was indeed
where he was, with Dinah up in the tree house.

"Well, at least he wasn't a joke anymore because of the centerfold," was the way a close
friend put it and it was true; people weren't
laughing anymore. What really got to Burt,
though, was that once again he'd made a "serious" movie, and once again he'd managed to
steal his own thunder. This time he couldn't
laugh it off, or make a wisecrack about it on the
TONIGHT show. The events in Gila Bend had
taken their toll. After relaxing in Florida, Burt
went into the hospital to have more corrective
surgery. He hadn't told anybody connected with
the film that after the first operation he'd been

forced to wear a truss for the remainder of the
shooting schedule. Dinah urged him to return to
the hospital as soon as possible, fearing even
worse complications if he were to put it off. It
was this second operation, following the first a
month earlier, which renewed speculation that he
was seriously ill. "Heart attack" and "cancer"
were whispered. It didn't help matters any when
Burt informed John Boorman with great regret
that he had to drop out of ZARDOZ, Burt's
next scheduled film. He'd received strict orders
from his doctors to take six weeks off and do
nothing but rest.

Boorman was deeply disappointed. He'd
wanted Burt for ZARDOZ in the hopes that another DELIVERANCE might emerge out of
their reunion. With Burt out of the picture,
ZARDOZ was temporarily shelved, only to be
revived later on by Boorman's signing of another
star to play the role originally written for Burt,
Sean Connery. Ironically, Connery would be re-
placing the actor who'd originally turned down
the opportunity to replace him as James Bond a
few years earlier.

The implications, however, of Burt's "illness"
were more serious than the gossip columnists
could hint at. It was one thing for the public to
fantasize Burt Reynolds playing Camille, but in
Hollywood, even the rumor of illness is a very
serious matter. Actors are employable on multi-
million dollar projects only if they're "insurable," meaning if the producers can get health
insurance covering the cost of a production
should a film be disrupted by a serious injury, or

death. James Dean was insurable only on condition he didn't drive while making GIANT. He was killed three days after production was finished, in a car crash. Montgomery Clift, one of the most gifted actors of his generation, was uninsurable in the last years of his drug- and booze-laced life and as a result couldn't find work in Hollywood. The real danger to Burt was that by not denying the rumors of his "impending death," he was in fact adding to their credibility.

He was finally tracked down by Dorothy Manners of the Los Angeles Herald-Examiner, who called him at the Jupiter ranch to find out the real story of his "mysterious illness."

"There's nothing mysterious about my illness," he told her. "It's simple. I just collapsed from exhaustion; the horrendous, physical and emotional strain that went with THE MAN WHO LOVED CAT DANCING immediately followed by surgery for a hernia." As for where his head was at, he added, "I'm not sorry for this time-out. I'm thinking, and beginning to realize a lot of things. . . .

"First, there's Dinah, an incredible lady. She's been fantastic through this whole thing. And now she's down here, riding and fishing and just sitting in the sun with me, trying to fatten me up with that marvelous cooking of hers. She's beautiful. I'm the luckiest guy in the world to have her. . . . Right now, well, lady, I got to go out and watch the sunset with Dinah, and take our little walk before dinner—man, are her dinners worth waiting for!"

Burt finally returned to Hollywood in June, only to discover that MGM was rush-releasing CAT DANCING. Aubrey dashed off a telegram to Burt "congratulating" him on his fine performance. The telegram did nothing to cool Burt's fury when Aubrey, in an attempt to boost initially disappointing box-office returns, okayed a new advertising campaign for the film. To Burt, it was obvious the audiences were staying away because they's been turned off by the scandal, not by the movie; that seemed logical. To Aubrey, it was just the opposite. The audience had to be reminded of the scandal. Therefore, MGM's ad campaign contained this screaming blurb: SEE BURT AND SARAH IN THE TORRID LOVE STORY THAT SHOCKED THE COUNTRY!

Burt angrily threatened to sue MGM if the ad wasn't pulled immediately. After hasty negotiations, MGM agreed to change the ad: SEE BURT AND SARAH IN *A* TORRID LOVE STORY THAT SHOCKED *THE OLD WEST!*

While THE MAN WHO LOVED CAT DANCING was being released, Merv Griffen approached Burt about the possibility of doing a documentary for television on himself. Burt agreed. Lew Grade had also been interested in using Burt as the host of a string of late-night weekend specials, tentatively titled THE LATE BURT REYNOLDS SHOW, slotted on the otherwise dead network time-slot of Saturday nights, 11:30 to 1:00 in the morning. Television always seemed a safe refuge to Burt, and he saw the Grade proposal as an opportunity to participate actively in the production end; something he still wanted to learn about, still with an eye to one day producing his own movies; a recurring dream that vacillated between fantasy and nightmare, depending on which off-screen disaster Burt was involved in at any given time. Forming a partnership with Henry Jaffee, Burt struck a deal with Lew Grade. Henry Jaffee was the ideal choice for Burt. A veteran of many years of television production, he was also Dinah's producer, responsible for the singer's long-term television talk-host career.

Meanwhile, film scripts were being hurled at him from all directions. After its shaky start, CAT DANCING was showing healthy box-office, and SHAMUS was an out and out smash. Burt was more in demand for movies than he'd ever been before, he could afford to pick and choose, and take his time to do it. After all, he'd made fifteen movies in seven years, and nearly every one had made huge profits. Even the stinkers, like NAVAJO JOE, eventually made money, mainly through continual re-release in the foreign markets, where American westerns could play forever.

After rejecting hundreds of awful scripts, finally one did catch his eye. Written by Tracy Keenan Wynn, from an original story by producer Al Ruddy, THE LONGEST YARD was an action-comedy built around a grudge-match football game played, in prison, between the guards and the inmates. What interested Burt in

THE LONGEST YARD was the same thing
that he'd picked up on in SEMI-TOUGH. He
was convinced that a film about football, if
handled correctly, could be a smash. To date,
there hadn't been a successful sports movie to
speak of, and at first glance a comedy about
football seemed, well, ludicrous rather than
witty. Yet, Burt, long searching for a script that
could unify his self-effacing good ol' boy TV
image with his tough, bare-chested macho big-
screen big-guy, saw the nucleus for such a film
in THE LONGEST YARD. He contacted Wynn
and told him he'd be interested, if Wynn would
agree to study Burt on TV, and to try to incor-
porate his natural comic vernacular into the
speech patterns of YARD's hero, Paul Crewe. In
other words, Burt wanted to play Burt Reynolds
in THE LONGEST YARD. Naturally, Wynn
agreed. With a deal set, Burt turned his attention toward blitzing TV with a series of shows so
successful they would redesign late-night programming for NBC. The LATE BURT REYN-
OLDS SHOW was the first step toward what
would eventually turn into SATURDAY NIGHT
LIVE, a show which would revolutionize Saturday night network programming, becoming so
successful it would be able to afford having Burt
Reynolds as its host one time. By proving you
could swing a little freer late at night and take
a few chances you might not take in regular
prime time, Burt managed to sustain his TV persona, and gain fantastic ratings.

It's probably no accident that the first show
was set inside a prison. Doing a remote from

Leavenworth served two purposes. First, it gave Burt the opportunity to get inside the walls of a high-security prison; a feat, by the way, that almost nobody else would have been able to pull off—a testimony to Burt's power, as well as his popularity, in television—and second, it planted the seeds for THE LONGEST YARD, which would return Burt to prison.

When interviewed by TV Guide about the prison special, Burt took a typical, self-effacing TV low profile: "Why did I decide to do it? I am not, essentially, a movie star," Burt confessed, being one of the top ten box-office draws notwithstanding. "I am essentially a TV personality," he continued. "I'll be doing what I love most of all; going out and putting myself on the line, warts and all, unrehearsed. If I could bring it off with those guys at Leavenworth—face it, Merle Haggard's their idol, not me, then I'd know I'd made the right decision." Hard and humble, that was the ticket. Including Merle Haggard as a guest was Burt's idea; a clever move, Haggard having done hard time at San Quentin before making it big as a Country star. On the other hand, having Dinah as a guest was something nobody could quite figure out. Most of all, Dinah, who didn't exactly feel at home singing to a captive audience of murderers, rapists and the like. Dinah was petrified at the thought of having to sing a duet with one "Big Jim," a lifer who practically drooled at the chance to sing with her—he'd been a prisoner since she'd been a teen swing band idol. Just before she was scheduled to go on, she turned to

"Big Jim," and said softly, "You'll have to par-
don me for being a little bit nervous because I've
never worked with anybody like you."

"Neither have I," Big Jim replied, grinning.

Surprisingly, things couldn't have gone smooth-
er while at Leavenworth; the cooperation between prisoners, guards, cast and crew was
nearly perfect, if the near escape of one drum-
mer and fifty cohorts could be dismissed as
overzealousness. The week the show was
scheduled to air, late October 1973, Burt made
the talk-show rounds to do some plugging. Enter-
ing through the stage door of the Philadelphia-
based Mike Douglas Show, Burt inadvertently
crossed a picket line, unaware that a strike by
IATSE (The International Alliance of Theatrical
State Employees) was in progress. One of the
pickets, infuriated, screamed an insult at Burt
relating to the *Cat Dancing* episode in Arizona.
Burt whirled and went for the guy. It took six
husky union pickets to keep him from tearing
the striking union member to pieces. The incident
was a haunting experience for Burt, recalling at
once the whole Gila Bend mess. Perhaps it made
him wonder if the public would ever let him forget.

Whatever the reasons, curiosity or devotion,
the prison show proved a ratings smash and
guaranteed the next five shows, scheduled far
enough apart to take him through most of
1974, up to the start of production on THE
LONGEST YARD. Each show was to have a

theme. The next one scheduled was "Bar Room Buddies," featuring Burt, Robert Mitchum, Peter O'Toole, and Jackie Gleason. Another was "The World's Greatest Lovers," starring Burt, Marcello Mastrionni, Sean Connery, Michael Caine, and Roger Moore. This was followed by a show built around Burt and "his women," a fantasy that would place the women of his dreams in their appropriate rooms in his house. While the bedroom and living room were filled, predictably with starlets, the kicker was that Burt put Dinah in the kitchen, presumably making one of those "great meals" for the whole gang.

NBC was so impressed with Burt that it offered his newly-formed production company four prime-time specials. As part of the deal, they would extend his late-night specials on a semi-regular basis. Burt agreed, if he didn't have to appear in all of them. He was anxious to get back to making movies. He was full of ideas, though, on how to fill his new TV time. One show would be a pilot for Wayne Newton, following Wayne and his friends around the Newton ranch, including a scene with Newton on horseback, singing a song in the desert. Another show would be a tribute to the Cotton Club, the famous Harlem nightspot, starring Lena Horne, Ray Charles, Jimmy Walker, Jonelle Allen, Aaron and Freddie, Cab Calloway, and O.C. Smith. Still another would be a show called "Why Oh Why Ohio," all about the famous comedians who came from that state; and another, a fantasy shot in Disney World, in which

Burt would appear to play a guy who didn't believe in Mickey Mouse or Donald Duck. "It's a show about how Disney World can change somebody," Burt eagerly explained to a reporter. Not all of his ideas made it to the tube.

Burt was busier than he'd ever been in his life and, as a result, seeing less and less of Dinah. Now, the never-ending statements to the press from the couple were beginning to take on a different tone. Whereas they'd always maintained, especially Burt, that age didn't matter between them, Dinah, in late '74, declared, "I can't picture myself growing old in Burt's arms." Further, Burt's friends knew that he'd always wanted to be a father. As far back as his marriage to Judy, he'd talked about having children. The inescapable truth was that, at fifty-five, Dinah was simply beyond child-bearing age.

While Dinah waited patiently for Burt to take a break, to relax, as his doctors kept telling him he needed to, he was busy preparing his last late-night special for NBC, a show he'd promised to the network before starting THE LONGEST YARD. This one was special in more ways than one; it was a labor of love for Burt—a tribute to stuntmen.

Naturally, Burt planned on featuring Hal Needham, his best friend, the guy he spent all his spare time with these days, spare time it seemed he didn't have for Dinah. Not that the boys were whooping it up or anything. This was just about the time when Needham's marriage was falling apart. Ironically, the day Needham packed his bags and moved out of his house, Burt offered to let Needham stay with him, rent-free, forever if he wanted. After all, it had meant a lot to Burt when Needham had made his place available when Burt's marriage had collapsed. Needham had, in fact, always been there, as far back as the "Gunsmoke" days when the tall, steel-breasted daredevil had taken the young Reynolds under his wing, teaching him how to take a fall—off a building, out of a marriage. When Burt had needed help escaping the media circus at the height of the Gila Bend lunacy, it was Needham who'd arranged his "escape." Now, Burt could pay him back, and with style. He'd just purchased a new house, George Harrison's ecstatic Bel-Air mansion which the former Beatle had shed in one of his transcendental anti-materialistic pouts.

Just as they complemented each other on screen, cinematically combining to create a single, heroic figure with the face and body of a Burt Reynolds extended heroically through the stunt magic of a Hal Needham, so did they roam the hills of Bel-Air, a couple of real-life Marlboro men sitting, dad, on top of the world. Individually, they were unique. Together, impenetrable.

Not that there was a total lack of company. For these two, the problem was never getting women. The problem was keeping them away. Recalled Needham when asked how it was when he first moved in with Burt: "Girls hung around the house like they used to for Elvis. They'd jump his car, try to bribe the pool man, the

laundry man. One girl came dressed from the gas
company, claiming she had to read the meter.
She didn't make it. Ladies always were coming
up to the gate phone and saying I have a gift for
Burt. I would always ask them if it were
wrapped." One time, late at night the burglar
alarms went off, tripped by an overzealous female "fan." Burt reached for his .38, always
nearby, and nearly shot the head off the girl before he caught a look at her legs. Things got so
crazy Burt and Hal took turns playing Burt.
When the tour busses would pass the house,
which seemed like every fifteen minutes, the
screams of the women could be heard all the way
in the backyard. One time Hal jumped into
Burt's Cadillac and drove past the bus, which
immediately took off after him. By the time
Needham got to the San Diego Freeway, there
was a caravan lined up behind him. Finally, the
bus caught up with the Cadillac, and one of the
women stuck her head through the window to
get a better look. "Hey," she said, somewhat disgruntled. "You're not Burt Reynolds!"

"Who said I was?" Needham replied, gunning
the Caddy and leaving the tourist line in his
dust. Far more annoying was the fact that no
matter how often Burt changed his phone number, and he was up to once a month, enterprising
young girls seemed somehow to get the new one
before he did and would call all hours of the day
and night.

So it seemed only fitting that Burt would devote his last TV special to his best friend, who'd
made a career out of doubling for his pal.

Once "The Stuntmen" was completed, Burt was ready for production to begin on THE LONGEST YARD. Traditionally, commencement was announced in the trades. Just about this time, another item appeared in the Hollywood dailies. Sarah Miles and her husband, Robert Bolt, had separated. Bolt would remain in England, while Sarah Miles had decided to relocate—to Hollywood.

sixteen

BURT chose Robert Aldrich to direct THE
LONGEST YARD. He liked Aldrich's movies,
particularly ATTACK and THE DIRTY DOZ-
EN. Aldrich, an ex-footballer, seemed to have
the right touch when it came to action. After
a couple of meetings, Burt felt confident that
Aldrich would be able to retain enough of the
good ol' boy in Burt's interpretation of Paul
Crewe to make the picture work. There was just
one thing Burt insisted on. The picture had to be
shot in Georgia. Burt was still turned off to Hollywood and New York. He believed he could
make movies away from the politics of the motion picture industry. In Hollywood, he was just
another actor making star demands. In Georgia,
he was practically a god, one of their own, returning to the promised land. And Florida was
only an anxiety-attack away.

Dinah? She'd have to stay behind in Hollywood, baking cookies on television. In spite of
all the rumors and the I-told-you-so's her so-
called friends were flinging at her, she bravely
smiled, even as word came flying west from
Georgia that Burt was carrying on with Ber-

nadette Peters, one of the co-stars of THE
LONGEST YARD. On the heels of the rumors,
Burt surprised Dinah by having a guilt-red
Maserati delivered to her front door. As soon as
she saw it, she called a contractor to build a garage around it. If she couldn't bury the rumors,
she could at least bury the car.

When Robert Aldrich told his star that
making THE LONGEST YARD in Georgia
presented production problems which could
prove to be insurmountable, Burt simply picked
up the telephone and called the governor, Jimmy
Carter, who was elated at the idea of having a
film shot in his state. He personally invited Aldrich and Georgia's new favorite son to the Governor's mansion to insure the state's full
cooperation. Aldrich estimates that Carter's actions saved the film a quarter of a million dollars
in production costs, making it feasible to be shot
entirely on location. Prison labor was used everywhere, and all ancillary expenses were picked
up by the state. The prisoners built a professional football stand inside the prison grounds at
Reedsville, complete with fences and grandstand,
where the final "big" game of the film was to be
shot. Aldrich recalls that first meeting with
Jimmy Carter: "The whole government shut
down for three hours. Everyone was watching
when we came out of the giant rotunda around
the governor's office. Those ladies down there
were really nuts about him. They were screaming
like it was back in Frank Sinatra's time. Burt
was great; charming. I never saw him refuse an
autograph. He stopped and took poses with old

ladies. He was very gracious."

THE LONGEST YARD is the story of a pro
football player expelled from the NFL for point
shaving, who takes out his frustrations by
beating up his girl friend and stealing her car, resulting in his arrest, conviction, and a season in
the state penitentiary. There he becomes involved in an intramural football game between
the prisoners and guards. The maniacal warden,
Eddie Albert, orders Burt to throw the game so
the guards will win. The climactic game becomes
a grueling physical contest between the black
shirts (the prisoners) and the white shirts (the
guards), as well as a psychological battle of wits
between Crewe and the Warden.

According to Aldrich, Burt was terrific to work
with, handily coordinating all phases of production, on-screen and off. The litmus test would
come, though, with the filming of the football sequence, a sequence that would run over forty
minutes on screen and would take six weeks of
shooting, six days a week. To intensify the action, Burt suggested hiring real football players
to fill out the two teams. Ray Nitschke of the
Green Bay Packers and Joe Kapp of the Min-
nesota Vikings were put in the Guards' front
line, directly opposite the black-shirted Burt,
and told not to hold back. The rest of the teams
were made up of semi-pros and even a couple of
prisoners. Burt even wore his old FSU number,
22.

The action on the field soon became more than
anyone had bargained for. The semis and the
cons were all out to prove something to the pros

and to the stars, looking for stories to tell their grandchildren—how I tackled Burt Reynolds, or broke Ray Nitchke's nose. After the first week, the black jerseys were no longer on speaking terms with the whites. One sequence, in particular, spelled out what was going on. A white shirt kept clipping Burt, an illegal move in pro ball, repeated time after time as the scene went through several re-takes. Before long, Burt was ready to kill the guy and might have taken a swing at him except for the fact that the guy outweighed him by sixty pounds, and Burt came up to the guy's chest. Still, take after take, Burt took the elbow and kept playing. Aldrich tells what happened next: "The rest of the guys loved Burt. They waited until . . . the third or fourth day, when we were getting down to do 'the longest yard.' I looked up and there was this guy just stretched out and the other guys were just walking away from him. I never asked, I never knew. It didn't come from the director, it didn't come from anybody. They just felt Burt was a regular guy who was trying real hard, even if he was a little too small for the part. I thought it was quite a testimonial to Burt."

If Burt had discovered his image in Hollywood, he was refining it in Georgia. No wonder Governor Carter rolled out the red carpet for Burt. THE LONGEST YARD not only provided a vehicle for Burt, it also created a new type of movie, the first of the phenomenally successful "good ol' boy" down-south films, whose quintessential star would forever stand at the pinnacle. Burt Reynolds was to the New South what John Wayne had been to the Old West, an icon whose very existence defined a genre.

THE LONGEST YARD was a box-office smash, proving to Burt that he could make movies his way, when he wanted, and where. And it was really only the beginning.

seventeen

WITH THE LONGEST YARD completed, Burt went directly into WW AND THE DIXIE-KINGS, feeling he owed Twentieth Century Fox a film after dropping out of ZARDOZ. While WW was in pre-production, Burt mapped out still another prime-time TV special, a Christmas '74 extravaganza to be shot on location at Boy's Town, starring Mickey Rooney, Bing Crosby, Perry Como, and Joe Namath. While he worked on the TV show, the WW script-writers worked on Burt's character, making sure that WW was essentially an extension of good ol' boy Gator McKlusky—different name, same charisma. Burt was sure he'd found his niche in films and the box-office returns seemed to confirm it. THE LONGEST YARD was proving to be a smash, after a sluggish start. At first, no one could figure why the film wasn't doing well, although the answer was obvious to Burt. The ad campaign for THE LONGEST YARD was selling the picture as a serious prison film. Burt suggested they change the ad emphasizing the comedy and the football. They did and the box-office soared, just one more indication to Burt that he was on the right track, in spite of reviews like those in *The New York Times*. Vincent Canby, the *Times'* film critic, wrote about Burt's performance in THE LONGEST YARD: "Reynolds may possibly be the phoniest love object to be foisted on the American public since the late Jayne Mansfield, and seems to have no personality of his own. It's not his fault that he looks so much like the early Brando, but it is a reflection of his talent as an actor that no matter how close the camera gets to him, he finds it difficult to convince you that he's thinking about anything except how to throw away the next line."

Canby, like most of the other critics, didn't have a clue as to what Burt's appeal was all about. He wasn't a love object at all. If anything, his image was that of the southern redneck with charm, who could easily kick sand in the face of the nearest male love-object and have the rest of the people on the beach love him for it. If the critics were looking for Cary Grant, they were trying to swim too deeply in shallow waters. Burt had been through the Hollywood star-mill ten years earlier and had been rejected, as much as he was rejecting the Hollywood system now. If Canby's piece, which really burned Burt up, had been about HAWK, or even DAN AUGUST, it might have made more sense.

Pauline Kael, on the other hand, seemed to catch on to what Burt was all about. In one of her New Yorker "think pieces," in 1974, she described Burt as the first major film star to have made it big via the television talk-show route. Essentially, she was suggesting, here's a guy who doesn't take himself very seriously, so why should we?

Leaving the critics to ponder his image, Burt took off for Nashville, to join the cast and crew for WW AND THE DIXIEKINGS, a combination Robin Hood and BONNIE AND CLYDE, southern style. WW rips off gas stations, sharing the loot with the station owners as a way of getting back at the bad-boy oil companies. While not exactly pulitzer material, WW gave Burt a lot of room to grin and crack one-liners while wrapping his arm around the voluptuous Connie Van Dyke, to laugh hysterically in that hyena cackle so familiar to his "Tonight Show" audience, to share a drink with Jerry Reed before punching out a few guys while a loud country music track blasted in the background.

And that was on-screen. At night, when the day's shooting was over, Burt would join Reed and Connie Van Dyke to hit the clubs. The friendship between Van Dyke and Burt soon became the main buzz among the crew of WW, so much so that when Dinah showed up one day— Nashville was her home-town and she was down to take care of some personal business—the tension on the set was quite noticeable. Rather than incorporating Dinah into the good-time atmosphere of the WW set, Burt went off with her, alone.

It was becoming clear to everyone, even Burt, that his relationship with Dinah was changing. Whatever reasons he'd had for pursuing her so ardently at first seemed to have receded, along with his passions. His relationship with his father was better than ever, his career was peaking, being accepted by his peers had now been augmented by international worship from adoring fans. The only thing lacking in his life, he confided to friends, was something he'd wanted for a long time—to be a father. Even during his marriage to Judy, having children was something he'd fantasized about. With Dinah in her midfifties, having a baby was, unfortunately, out of the question. Which is why almost everyone was sure than when Burt announced his intention to adopt, it also meant he was going to ask Dinah to marry him, to become the mother of his children.

Or at least he thought he was going to adopt. Agency after agency turned down his applications, usually citing his "lifestyle" as the reason. Being divorced didn't help either. His image as a womanizer might kill any attempts of his ever being able to adopt a child.

If there had been tension between Burt and Dinah before, Burt's failure to adopt children didn't make things any better. Burt flashed angry when he appeared on "The Today Show," being interviewed by Barbara Walters to plug THE LONGEST YARD. Things started off well enough, with Walters on familiar territory, asking Burt why he "hid" himself on the Cosmo centerfold photo with his hand. "Arm, Barbara, arm," was Burt's clever, dead-pan reply. He wasn't quite so dead-pan, though, when Walters asked about rumors of the break-up between Burt and Dinah. "That's a pretty stupid question. You wouldn't want me to ask you how you felt about your divorce, would you?" Burt replied, uncharacteristically testy on the airwaves.

With WW AND THE DIXIEKINGS in the can, Burt went directly into Peter Bogdanovitch's AT LONG LAST LOVE, a totally improbable choice of films and one of his few box-office disasters. Robert Aldrich, anxious to work with Burt again, was mystified by it. "I think Bogdanovitch had a spell over Burt and that spell could make Burt do anything. AT LONG LAST LOVE was not one of Burt's best efforts." Still others saw LOVE as Burt's way of playing with Bogdanovitch's long-time live-in, the mischievously sexy Cybill Shepherd. By any standards, though, making the movie was a career blunder. After disdaining the tinsel of Hollywood for the soul of the South; after finally breaking away from the manufactured gloss of the sound stages in favor of the fertilized fields of Georgia, Burt made an abrupt turnaround going into a Hollywood musical by a director who'd never done one before, starring not a single legitimate singer or dancer in the entire cast! Dressed in a tux, top hat and cane, Burt looked as comfortable tap-dancing as John Wayne would have dancing the Dying Swan. Dubbed "At Long Last Lousy" by one critic, the film all but ended Cybill Shepherd's film career and put the skids on the big-budget whims of Bogdanovitch. Oblivious to the disaster-in-the-making, Bogdanovitch and company had a ball. Bogdanovitch even hosted "The Tonight Show" during production, getting the assignment to sub

for Johnny on Burt's personal recommendation.
Bogdanovitch opened the show doing a bad impersonation of Cary Grant, then introduced his
two guests, Burt and Cybill, who all but openly
petted on the couch. Pretending to be annoyed
and upset, Bogdanovitch urged Burt and Cybill
to take it easy, which of course encouraged the
two of them to step up their actions. While most
people wrote off the show as one long plug for
LOVE, there were those who felt that a genuine
rift had developed that night between Bogdanovitch and Burt over Cybill; a rumor that would
gain credence when Bogdanovitch would fail to
show up to present Burt with the 1974 Enter-
tainer of the Year Award, as he was scheduled to
do. Although a rift did in fact develop between
the two, it didn't come to a head until NICK-
LEODEON, a film they made together in 1976.
Bogdanovitch's absence from the award presentation had less to do with any personal animos-
ities as it did with the FBI.

LOVE was shooting that day at San Marino,
just south of Santa Monica. Bogdanovitch had
devised a special electronic apparatus which en-
abled him to transmit, via FM, the soundtrack
for the film to cast members wearing special ear
plugs, allowing them to synchronize their musical numbers to the previously recorded track.
The only trouble with the scheme was that
Bogdanovitch was broadcasting AT LONG
LAST LOVE on an unauthorized frequency,
being picked up by government agents, who
couldn't make head or tails of what they were
monitoring. Tracing the signal to San Marino,

they raided the set as if they were on a major drug bust. The only one who escaped the invasion was Burt, who'd left earlier that day to prepare for his award dinner at the Beverly Wilshire Hotel in Beverly Hills, resulting in his picture and fingerprints being the only ones not taken by the FBI.

The only other incident worth mentioning in connection with LOVE was Burt's collapse during the shooting of one particularly vigorous dance sequence. Ever since CAT DANCING, rumors hinted of Burt's poor health with "bad heart" leading the pack. This last spell resulted in his being rushed, not to the hospital but to Dinah's place, where she came flying directly from New York, arriving at 4:00 A.M. to make and feed him chicken soup. LOVE shut down for a week while Burt was nursed by Dinah, who was always ready to take care of him. All he had to do was call. Or faint.

By early 1975, Burt returned to his senses, and to Aldrich, to start working on HUSTLE, a film he'd agreed to do if he could officially co-produce. Aldrich was all for it. After all, Burt had just been named to the Top Ten Box-Office Star list for the second time in a row, placing number six for the year 1974.

Here is Robert Aldrich's version of how HUSTLE was put together: "HUSTLE was brought to me by Burt. I liked the property but I didn't like the story. So Burt and I bought an option on the property and formed a company called Robrick Productions. We paid $25,000

against the production. I persuaded Burt that
the love relationship would not work with an
American girl, that American mores being what
they are, nobody is really going to apprehend or
endorse a love story with a prostitute. However,
it would work if she were a foreigner, particularly if she were French. That morality is for-
given. I made a condition the girl had to be
French, and the first major casting. I wanted
Catherine Deneuve. Burt wasn't sure she should
be foreign and wasn't that crazy about having
Deneuve. We went to Paris, had two meetings
with her, and found her very calculating; a very
bright lady. She wanted a week to think about it.
Burt said he wasn't about to sit there for a week
so he went back to the States. I had outlined to
Burt what I considered to be the missing elements in the script, in terms of scenes missing
between him and Deneuve. He agreed, but said
we shouldn't bring it up until after Deneuve decided to do the picture. A week went by, she
came to America, we had lunch and she agreed
to do the picture; if A, B, and C changes were
made. It so happened she wanted the same
changes Burt and I wanted.

"Then the writer didn't want to make the
changes, so we had to get somebody else to do
them. The writer became indignant, causing
more delays, but we finally got the problems
worked out. The nature of the changes were the
reasonableness of a lady of leisure saying to an
American lover if you take care of me I'll quit
being a hustler. This put a mild dilemma on the
man. In the picture Burt has an ex-wife and

child. He's not emotionally capable of considering a matrimonial role with a prostitute. If he's in love with her, he certainly ought to be capable of saying I'll take care of you. The problem with the picture is, can a conventional, middle-class American bring himself to say that? What happened in the movie was that he was a schmuck. He decided she was good enough to take care of, but before he could take her to San Francisco he got himself killed. Having him killed was something Deneuve insisted on.

"We made a lot more money on HUSTLE than anybody thought. Burt probably took, above his salary, another million and a half out of that picture. I think Burt was exceptionally good in it. It's not an upper, though, it's a downer, and as a consequence, when people talk about Burt Reynolds pictures it's not at the top of the hit list. There's no Chevrolets going through Georgia."

There's little doubt, though, as to what attracted Burt to HUSTLE. The nearly $3 million in salary and percentage would keep his name on the Top Ten Box-Office list, especially after the AT LONG LAST LOVE disaster. Even more important, though, was that HUSTLE had given Burt a chance to inch ever closer to the autonomous mini-mogul stature he so coveted; a time when he would make Burt Reynolds movies, and only Burt Reynolds movies, without ever having to step inside a Hollywood studio again. As for the rumors which came out of Paris that Burt and Deneuve were having a torrid love affair, Aldrich tells quite a different tale: "Miss Deneuve was somewhat less than overwhelmed by America's favorite good ol' boy. I suspect that he thought he was going to prove to be more attractive to Miss Deneuve than he actually was. He'd not been confronted with her kind of worldliness before. To her, he was just another leading man. This lady had a lot of mileage, and I think that impressed him. They worked marvelously together. As for the womanizing, I never saw it."

In spite of his dealings with Deneuve, control was something Burt was proving to be quite good at. When a friend pointed out that the infamous COSMO centerfold picture was now on the cover of MOTION PICTURE magazine, Burt promptly sued Francesco Scavullo, who may have figured since he took the pictures he had a right to the negatives, a direct violation of the contractual agreement Burt had made with Helen Gurley Brown. Scavullo, conceding he'd acted without permission, settled the case out of court by paying an undisclosed amount to Burt and handing over all the remaining session negatives.

The only copy of the photo that Burt allowed to be reproduced after that was the one he had made into a dartboard, with the bullseye you-know-where, hanging in what he dubbed "The Ego Room," so lettered in gold leaf on the front door of the den in the new Bel-Air mansion. In addition to the dartboard, the room's walls were covered floor to ceiling with photos of every stage of his career.

There were also pictures of his prized Appaloosas, another facet of the burgeoning Reynolds empire. A retail store had recently been opened down on the ranch to accommodate the endless stream of tourists who made The Reynolds Horse Ranch the second most popular attraction in Florida, just behind Disney World. The first day the souvenir store opened, 7,000 people jammed through its doors, buying everything that had the initials BR, or a picture of Burt, on it. As for his prized Appaloosas, two of the first three entered in quartertrack championship races came in first.

Control was also the heart of the matter, as far as Dinah was concerned. Burt knew, finally, it was time to cut the apron strings. He had a choice. He could leave things as they were forever, or he could play it straight. He had no choice, really. He respected Dinah far too much to drag her any further through the rumor mills, which would continue to have a field day every time he looked at another woman. And looking wasn't the only thing he was interested in doing.

As soon as he told Dinah it was over, he went through agonizing second thoughts, constantly reaching for the phone, stopping himself with a drink, or a popper—amyl nitrate—or by running through the backfield of women lined up like the Dallas Cowboy Cheerleaders waiting, for Burt to make good on his promise; the same promise he made to all of them, to call again soon, which of course he never did. The faces and bodies were interchangeable. Starlets, secretaries, stewardesses. One or two of the young actresses he dated during this period actually broke through and went on to stardom. One wound up as his co-star, a couple of years later, reminding him, at their first meeting, that he'd never called back, as he'd "promised."

The newspapers, meanwhile, still unaware that Burt and Dinah had split, were having a field day. Trying to rationalize Burt's attachment to Dinah in the midst of all his playing around, fantastic stories began to "emerge" that Burt's "penchant" for older women was the result of his first sexual experience at the age of fourteen with a woman of thirty-five. For his part, Burt felt no obligation to the press. As long as Dinah understood their relationship, that was enough. She would never be humiliated as long as he didn't deceive her.

Perhaps it was because he'd been so straight with her. Whatever the reason, Burt and Dinah remained close friends, constantly in touch. When Burt became involved, briefly, with Lorna Luft, Liza Minelli's kid sister, it was with Dinah's official blessing. And it was into Dinah's arms Burt went for consolation when he broke up with Lorna, who sought her own consolation with Mac Davis.

Early in 1975, Burt began to work on Stanley Donen's LUCKY LADY, and the rumor machines cranked up for another merciless assault on "poor" Dinah, sitting at home while Burt was flying high with his latest co-star, Liza Minelli. This last press campaign was too much, prompting Burt to release an "official statement" to the press that he and Big "D" had officially split up as lovers but would always remain friends.

If his forthright statement to the press about his relationship with Dinah took away some of their ammunition, he reloaded their guns quickly enough. LUCKY LADY was being shot on location, in Guaymas, Mexico, the same town Mike Nichols used to film CATCH-22, and it was in Guaymas that Burt announced his intention to lend his "sumptuous penthouse suite" to a group of women meeting in Mexico City as part of the United National International Woman's Year. "I'm surprised and pleased that they asked me," Burt said. "It's a misconception that I'm not in favor of women's lib; I'm very much in favor and have been trying to get them to take off their bras for years. . . ."

LUCKY LADY was another short circuit in Burt's career. Playing against type, he came across in this 1920's ascot comedy as stiff and bored. The self-effacing image that usually worked so well came across, in LUCKY LADY as smarmy arrogance, with all the subtle shading of a morning-after face in a well-lit bathroom mirror. The Reynolds pattern of taking a giant step forward in dungarees and one backward in tuxedo and tinsel was in force once again. LUCKY LADY was another financial disaster at the box office, following the successful HUSTLE, which had followed the disastrous AT LONG LAST LOVE, which had followed the successful WW AND THE DIXIEKINGS and THE LONGEST YARD.

LUCKY LADY was filled with grim days of shooting down in sweaty Mexico, where Donen's British crew treated the locals with total contempt. "Somewhere along the way," Burt told a reporter, "the film bogged down because the totally wrong man directed it. He was so lost out there in the water with all those boats, guns, planes, and things going off." In fact, the only popular figure on the set was Burt, who felt perfectly at home along the Mexicans; far more than he did among the British. Gene Hackman, Burt's co-star, was so ill at ease that he had provisions in his contract for a private plane to be on call, to take him back to the United States if he was not to be used for more than one day's shooting. Why would Burt make a movie as dismal as LUCKY LADY? One reporter asked him that question and got this straightforward answer: "It's geared to make money—and being the crass commercial person that I am, it seemed right to me from the beginning and it got better as the people got involved and the chemistry started working." Aside from the latter part of the statement hyping the "chemistry," the part about the money was where the action was for Burt, who was no doubt looking to build a fund for his producing ventures by lending his face out to the highest bidder.

LUCKY LADY's forgettable plot centered around a robbery, STING-style, a film whose tremendous success no doubt spawned LUCKY LADY and a host of other "clever" robbers-with-charm films. Set aboard a sailing ship, much of the action was shot on the sixty-foot deck, with more than fifty crew people and several tons of equipment aboard at all times. Liza Minelli termed the shooting circumstances "ridiculous," but Burt summed it up best. "I would estimate that this picture saved me about $70,-000. I know now I'll never buy a sailing boat, yacht, houseboat, rowboat, or canoe." Maybe it was that $70,000 he saved that he decided to put into THE POSH BAGEL, the bagel store he opened smack in the middle of Beverly Hills. With LUCKY LADY completed, Burt threw a gigantic opening day party at THE POSH BAGEL, inviting all his Hollywood friends in for some cream cheese and lox, Southern-Jewish style.

No sooner had the butter melted on the first onion bagel than Burt left the hills of Beverly for the plains of Georgia, where GATOR was about ready to roll. GATOR was Burt's first sole venture into producing. He'd chosen his material well. GATOR, the sequel to the highly successful WHITE LIGHTNING, was the continuation of the adventures of Gator McKluskey, and the first legitimate good ol' boy film Burt would be in since WW AND THE DIXIEKINGS. It was time, he knew, to get back to his roots.

In addition to producing GATOR, Burt decided to take a chance on a new director—himself. Having not directed anything since the last episodes of "Hawk," he decided it was time to gain another firm grip on the controls of the burgeoning Burt Reynolds movie industry. Since WW, films had become big business down South. Nearly forty good ol' boy movies were now slated for production; with membership in the southern branch of the Screen Actors Guild doubling in the last few years. Every southern politician had taken his cue from Jimmy Carter and had formed film commissions to lure production companies, and their endless stream of dollars, to "come on down." More and more, independent productions heeded the call. Along with the built-in incentives every southern state was willing to throw in, such as free labor, no-hassle location shooting, and lots of non-union technicians, there were unmistakable signs at the box-office that red-neck adventures made box-office gold. The southern hero was something new to American moviegoers, the opposite of the typical Hollywood leading man. Perhaps the movement away from the Cary Grants and the Clark Gables began in the fifties, with the brooding anti-heroics of Brando and Dean who, while being rebellious in nature, embodied that rebellion pretty-boy style. Hollywood was still mesmerized by the faces of beautiful women and pretty men, the essence of the American hero and the woman he loved.

Ah, but the southern heroes were different. "Swamp-smart," Burt called them: "Good ol' boys who fight the system with dignity and, above all, a sense of humor. The men want to be like him. The women want to be with him." It didn't take independent producers long to realize that fortunes could be made by plucking anonymous Johnny Rebs from the cotton fields and building films around them—lots of action, fistfights, car chases, and lots of leering sex to keep it truly vulgar.

Such was the case with a little number called PREACHERMAN, a film made in 1975 for $65,000 by a then obscure Charlotte, North Carolina movie distributor, Robert D. McClure. By rounding up a couple of backers, renting minimal equipment, and using non-union technicians and actors, in sixteens days McClure filmed what amounted to two hours of car chases, some moonshine comedy, fat and dumb sheriffs held hostage by their own ignorance, and the film went on to gross $5 million—*without playing a single major city north of the Carolinas!* PREACHERMAN was a revelation to the film industry, but old news to Burt, who'd known for a long time there was a large, untapped population in America which didn't read *The New York Times* or *Variety* and was willing to spend their bucks regardless of what Vincent Canby thought. On the heels of PREACHERMAN came ODE TO BILLY JOE, RETURN TO BOGIE CREEK, MACON COUNTY LINE, and WALKING TALL. "They're not Shakespeare," Burt said of the new southern genre he had created. "Not that I wouldn't like to play Shakespeare one day. . . . Heck, I might even like to do a Walt Disney!" There was little doubt left in Hollywood that if Burt put on a pair of big, floppy ears and chased Minnie Mouse for two hours it would be a hit, as long as it was shot and shown down south.

* * *

Late in 1975, Burt Reynolds was invited to host a black-tie party to celebrate the 20th anniversary roast of Hal Needham, now the highest paid stuntman in Hollywood. Held at Tony Duquette's West Hollywood studio, the party proved to be a smash affair. All of Burt's pals showed up, including Dinah, who provided the best line of the evening, when she assured the audience that in spite of the fact that Hal Needham was Burt's favorite stand-in, "I can say for sure that Hal doesn't always double for Burt."

The only down note of the evening was the last-minute cancellation by John Wayne, slated to co-host the affair with Burt. South was not to meet West that night, for the Duke was forced to cancel his appearance due to a nagging cold. Sending a wire to Burt, he seemed to echo in a few words what was, in effect, the sentiment of the Hollywood establishment toward the new, radical anti-studio band of good ol' boys tossing their own "do" right here in enemy territory. Apologizing for not being able to attend, Wayne ended his telegram informing Burt and Needham not to worry, "I'll be around to bury you both."

eighteen

By 1976, Burt was number six on the Top Ten Box-Office List, while Wayne's last appearance, at number ten, had been as far back as 1974 (the last year The Duke would ever make the list). However, Burt still wasn't satisfied. Having virtually created a new arm of the motion-picture industry—the southern good ol' boy film having conquered the skeptics who'd told him long ago to give it up, he had no talent—he told *The New York Times*, "I could walk away from the adulation as an actor and never miss it. I'd much rather be a chess player than a chess pawn." Explaining he had new worlds to conquer, directing, for instance, Burt told *The Times*, "There is just so long that I can go on jumping out of windows, off cliffs and over cars. Since no one was offering me the kind of roles I wanted to play, I felt I had to go into another area. I desperately wanted to do ONE FLEW OVER THE CUCKOO'S NEST, but they went with the guy who had been nominated for an Oscar the year before and had won the New York Critics Award. I think Jack Nicholson was brilliant in the movie; I just wish I had the chance to be equally brilliant."

If Burt was bitter about Nicholson's success, he had a right to be. After all, their careers hadn't been all that different. Nicholson had spent years in Hollywood making pseudo-psychedelic motorcycle movies in the sixties for Roger Corman, going nowhere real fast until he hit it big in Peter Fonda's hippie, idiosyncratic EASY RIDER, a picture that anticipated Burt's SMOKEY AND THE BANDIT by some ten years. A road picture, and an independent production, EASY RIDER was a one-shot phenomenon, a film supposed to die for lack of distribution that broke all box-office records. It particularly rankled Burt that Nicholson, who'd placed two notches behind him on the Top Ten list in '74, was being touted as the new kid in town, complete with an oscar nomination, while Burt still carried the tag as glorified stuntman who couldn't act his way out of a paper script.

Perhaps one reason Burt continued to receive the cold shoulder was that Hollywood, forever a bottom-line industry town, saw him as a rebel, and rebellion usually meant uncertain box-office. Sure, Nicholson had hit it big with EASY RIDER, but once established, he was more than eager to make traditional Hollywood movies, to play by the rules. Burt, though, continued to take his show on the road, to pull money and attention away from Hollywood and into the South, giving birth to a whole new genre of movie making that kicked southern sand in Malibu's face. Worse, he continued to poke fun at himself and the industry in public. Nicholson might give serious interviews about his "technique," and his "commitment," but Burt preferred to go on "The Tonight Show" giggling about movies and women, while continuing to raise hell in the South producing and directing films like GATOR.

Winding up post-production on GATOR, Burt was amused to read that NBC was putting "Hawk" back into prime-time, rerunning the ten-year-old series the way ABC had recently done with "Dan August." In 1966, "Hawk" was as stylistically out-of-date as the toupee Burt wore while making it, yet it was strong enough to outpoint its first-run competition, leaving the network wishing it had a hundred more episodes of the series it had so quickly canceled. Burt was beseiged with offers from all three major networks to star in a series, any series, Burt Reynolds in The Phone Book, just name your price.

The moment had passed, though, and everyone knew it. Oh, he might still drop in on Johnny, and for some reason he got a kick out of doing "Hollywood Squares," but that was it. So desperate were producers for new Burt Reynolds product that someone got the rights to his one-liners from the game show and released an album called "Zingers from the Hollywood Squares." And it didn't do all that badly.

In spite of the continual lack of awards and nominations—Hollywood's way of punishing him for being a wise guy—he was highly in demand

for pictures, his name above the title virtually
guaranteeing big box office. He agreed to make
NICKLEODEON for Peter Bogdanovitch when
he called, asking Burt to do the film as a personal favor. Bogdanovitch had fallen out of favor since his wunderkind LAST PICTURE
SHOW days. Not only AT LONG LAST LOVE,
but also DAISY MILLER, another Bogdanovitch film, had bombed. Bogdanovitch was living
proof of the old Hollywood adage that a director
was only as good as his last bottom-line.

NICKLEODEON was to be an ode to silent
movies. However, Bogdanovitch's once-sweet
charm had turned sour, causing tension on the
set and off. The rumored on-again off-again
Bogdanovitch-Cybill Shepherd romance was
rumored off-again, reportedly because the studio
had allegedly forbidden Bogdanovitch to make
NICKLEODEON if his blond paramour appeared in so much as one foot of it. The rumored
on-again Reynolds-Shepherd romance, meanwhile, was rumored on-again, making things
even uneasier. Then, one morning, during a particularly physical piece of business, Burt turned
to look off-camera. With eyes unfocused, and a
face full of cold water, he collapsed.

The word flashed through Hollywood that
Burt had had a heart attack/was on the verge of
having a heart attack/was reportedly recovering
from a heart attack/had been dead for weeks.
Meanwhile, the doctors at the hospital where
Burt had been rushed could find nothing wrong
with him. Submitting him to test after test, they

patted him on the back and sent him on his way, smiling, telling him to take it easy.

Burt felt too weak to continue shooting. He asked Bogdanovitch if it were possible to get some time off. No problem, Bogdanovitch assured him, they could shoot around him for two weeks, using Hal Needham for the long shots. Burt went home to rest and calm down, but nearly exploded when someone close to the action told him Bogdanovitch had reported Burt's "illnesses" to the producers and was collecting insurance money on him. Bogdanovitch heatedly denied this, but even the rumor of insurance trouble could be devastating to a career. Uninsurable meant unemployable. There were varying opinions as to what had actually taken place. Some felt that perhaps Bogdanovitch was out for revenge because of the Burt-Shepherd "affair," while others felt that Bogdanovitch was retaliating for what he considered Burt's delaying the movie.

Whatever the truth actually was, the rumors of insurance problems were as stubborn as the pains in Burt's chest. Finally, in an effort to put them to rest once and for all, he submitted to a full battery of tests to satisfy the insurance company. He even went so far as to submit to a heart catherization, one of the most painful tests imaginable in which a tube is inserted into an artery in the arm and slowly inched up to the heart.

With that ordeal behind him, he was given the official okay to return to NICKLEODEON, which he did chewing Valium and Seconal to

slow his heart beat and prevent another "attack," either to his heart, or Bogdanovitch's
face.

With NICKLEODEON finished, Burt immediately went into production on SMOKEY AND
THE BANDIT, a raunchy, good ol' boy film
concerning the misadventures of a seedy truck-
driving hero and his dealings with a local police
chief, to be shot on location, naturally, in Atlanta, Georgia. Originally, SMOKEY was a
throwaway, a favor to Hal Needham squeezed
between two "major" Burt Reynolds pictures,
NICKLEODEON and the upcoming SEMI-
TOUGH, the football property and stillborn
Broadway musical. (David Merrick, having seen
Burt in THE LONGEST YARD now agreed
that yes, Burt was Billy Clyde after all.)

"Every single one of my advisors and friends
went down on their knees, begging me with tears
in their eyes not to make SMOKEY," Burt told
one reporter. In addition, his doctors were warning him to slow down, to stop piling films one on
top of the other without a break. However,
Needham was having trouble convincing a studio
he could direct, understandable since his only
previous experience was as a stuntman. So Burt
personally took SMOKEY to the studio heads to
try and convince them to let Needham have a
shot. Fine, one studio finally said, we'll let Needham direct, as long as you play The Bandit.

Which is how it happened that Burt found
himself back at Universal, seventeen years after
having been fired from the studio for having no
talent.

Burt personally supervised all aspects of SMOKEY. After all, he'd put his reputation on the line backing Needham. If the film failed, it would be on Burt's shoulders, everyone knew that. He wanted Jackie Gleason to play the Sheriff, that one was easy. Not so easy was the critical role of The Frog, The Bandit's girl friend. Burt finally settled on a young actress with only one flop film to her credit, one TV mini-series still to be aired, and three sit-coms made around the time of Burt's 'Gunsmoke"-"Hawk"-"Dan August" days.

Burt's choice was Sally Field, TV's Gidget and Flying Nun. According to Hal Needham, "She was an interesting little twerp at the time. I taught her how to chew tobacco." He recommended her to Burt because she had "a cute figure and can get into almost any feeling you want—as quick as you want." Also Field reminded Burt of something he saw in himself. As he put it, "I thought she felt trapped inside this image people had of her in this town."

Field's TV career came to a grinding halt after her third series, "The Girl With Something Extra," an amalgam of "Gidget," "The Flying Nun," and "Bewitched," co-starring John Davidson, was canceled. Shortly after the network dropped her she and her husband divorced, leaving her with two children to raise. Her story was a familiar one in Hollywood. Landing the role in "Gidget" at the age of seventeen, and taking off with "The Flying Nun" at nineteen, she was America's sweetheart, her face on every magazine cover. She seemed able to balance a marriage and a career without so much as getting a pimple. Fabulously successful at twenty, she found herself washed up at twenty-five, unable to get work after "The Girl With Something Extra."

Five years passed. It was 1975 when Zohra Lambert, an actress who'd worked with Sally on "The Girl With Something Extra," recommended her to a casting director looking for a sexy southern receptionist type for Bob Rafelson's new movie, STAY HUNGRY. Rafelson's reaction to Sally Field was the same as the casting director's—You must be kidding!—nevertheless she got the part. Now she was assured by her agent, her manager and their secretaries that her career was sure to take off.

It didn't. STAY HUNGRY starved at the box office, and Sally returned to her children. Her agent continued to send her up for parts, and eventually Sally landed the role of SYBIL, another "Girl With Something Extra," in this case sixteen personalities. Her interpretation of the schizophrenic teenager would eventually win her an emmy. However, before the show was aired, with her career still in limbo, her thoughts were on remodeling her house.

One day, in the middle of studying some blueprints, she received a phone call from her agent. Burt Reynolds was asking if Sally would consider making SMOKEY AND THE BANDIT. Her first instinct was to say no, then and there. Burt Reynolds pictures were not her type of movie. She agreed to read the script at her agent's urging, which he sent right over. Her first instinct had been right. SMOKEY was the worst thing she'd ever read. She called her agent to say no, she wasn't interested. Her agent told her she ought to call Burt back in person, out of courtesy. Call Burt? That cowboy? She'd heard all about how crazy he was, and she was scared to death of him! Her hand shook as she dialed his number. "Sally Field? This is Burt Reynolds, star!"

"Oh, yeah? And this is Glenda Jackson." That broke the ice, as they both found themselves laughing out loud. They talked for a while, each liking the sound of the other's voice. Finally, Burt asked if she'd read the script. "Well, Mr. Reynolds, I don't want to be offensive, but I don't think it's all that good."

"I know," Burt said, smooth and unshaken. "It's awful, but trust me. We'll have a great time." An hour later, Sally called her agent to say she would accept the role.

She arrived in Atlanta in August of 1976, expecting Burt to greet her at the airport with flowers. In fact, Burt was still in Hollywood, purposely finding reasons to stay away from Atlanta until Sally arrived, not wanting to meet her in person. He preferred to call her on the phone from the hotel when he arrived, the next day, to ask her for a date. It was patented Reynolds—don't show up, jump out of a spice closet, gain the upper hand. Sure, Sally said, I'll meet you. If she was casual on the phone, she was hysterical once she hung up. "My body was raw

from changing clothes," she'd recall later. She
spent hours getting dressed, finally settling on
black velvet pants, high heels, and an orange em-
broidered Mexican shirt. Ready three hours
early, she spent the time writing to herself in her
diary. "You're good, Sally, a wonderful person.
He's no better than you are."

She tried so hard to be cool. She talked like a
truck driver, using every swear word she'd ever
heard, even those she didn't understand. She
called the food dirty names. She figured she
could keep it up forever if she had to; this was
obviously what Burt had in mind. Although the
charade lasted for days, Burt saw through it immediately. He'd chosen Sally for that same "You
must be kidding" reaction Bob Rafelson had.
The trouble now was that he didn't know how to
break through her bravado without breaking her
spirit. Two things were clear to Burt. She was
going to be perfect as The Frog, and damnit,
he'd fallen for her.

On the third day of shooting, in a scene between The Frog and The Bandit, in The Bandit's
black Trans-Am, Burt turned to her between
takes and said, simply, "I know this is not the
way you are. You have a tremendous amount to
offer just by being yourself. You don't need to
do this." Sally broke down, sobbing in relief. It
was, as Burt would later describe it, "the beginning, middle, and end of the start of a relationship."

*   *   *

If there were indications in his earlier good ol'
boy films that Burt was trying to make a statement about his own life, SMOKEY AND THE
BANDIT WAS rife with autobiographical paral-
lels. First there was the continuing conflict between a popular but rebellious bandit played by
Burt and a tough, rambunctious-with-a-heart-
of-gold sheriff, Smokey, played by Jackie
Gleason. Further, the sheriff has an idiot-son as
a partner, constantly getting in the way of his
catching up with the bandit. It's not that difficult
to see the relationship between the sheriff's son
and the bandit as representing two extremes of
Burt—the early, self-destructive actor with two
attitudes, mad and madder, and the latter-day
public hero who can do no wrong; both relating,
in their way, to the father-sheriff figure. Then
there's Sally Field, as The Frog, sitting alongside
The Bandit as Sally would be alongside Burt.
The most interesting aspect of The Bandit/Burt
correlation, though, is the image of The Bandit
as he sees himself—a lovable charlatan, a kind of
Evel Kneivel who drinks too much, fights too
much, puts down women, breaks the law, yet is
somehow redeemed by his charm. In many ways,
SMOKEY AND THE BANDIT is the ultimate
good ol' boy movie, bringing all the elements of
southern tradition into clashing focus with the
mythic, rebellious, anti-heroics of the new
South, represented as legitimately by Burt Reynolds in SMOKEY as it would be by Jimmy
Carter in politics, Terry Bradshaw in sports, and
Willie Nelson in music.

In many ways, SMOKEY is the realization of

elements introduced in Burt's first directorial effort, GATOR. Both films are rural, southern adventures. Both have soundtracks and title tunes
by Jerry Reed, a country singer who also
acts in GATOR and SMOKEY. Both films
personify "The Law" as a bloated, ineffectual,
seedy, urban "villain"—Jack Weston in GATOR,
Jackie Gleason in SMOKEY. Hal Needham,
SMOKEY's director, was the second-unit director for GATOR, responsible for shooting the se-
quences in which the first-unit director, Burt,
appeared. Since Burt is in almost every shot of
GATOR, Needham had ample opportunity to
learn his craft.

Both films introduce Burt the same way;
relaxed, stretched out, smiling. Cut to a close-up,
to Burt laughing in that high, siren-whine so
familiar to "Tonight Show" audiences, and it's
off to the races.

The crucial difference, though, between GA-
TOR and SMOKEY is the dispensing of plot in
SMOKEY AND THE BANDIT. With GATOR,
there is still a vestige of "seriousness." Gator is
coerced by the law to go underground in order to
prevent his father from being put in jail for
moonshining. Gator's mission is to catch the bad
guys in order to save the good ones. In
SMOKEY, there simply are no bad guys. The
subject again is bootlegging—the illegal interstate truck-running of beer—the flimsiest of pre-
texts for two hours of car stunts and fist fights in
which absolutely nobody ever gets hurt. If the
pressure is off the characters, it's also off the audience. The only message left in SMOKEY is

hey, y'all, relax, take your shoes off, set awhile, have a beer, put your arm about your gal or guy, and have a good time. Substitute a horse for a Trans-Am, and it's Satursay night at the Bijou, anywhere USA, starring Tom Mix, or Johnny Mack Brown, or even the Duke himself.

"Producer Bob Evans said I'd proved more with SMOKEY than with anything else," Burt told the Los Angeles Times. "Kirk Douglas told me he saw the film five times. And he didn't apologize, like most people do. Most people say, 'I didn't want to go, but the kids made me. . . .' I don't know where that patronizing attitude comes from. Maybe from that centerfold business. Maybe from my early work. . . . Today I look at the camera as someone I've been having an affair with for the past twenty years and who's only just realized how good in bed I am."

SMOKEY AND THE BANDIT would go on to gross more than $200 million *domestically*—not counting foreign rentals, cable and broadcast TV rights—making it the second highest grossing film of 1977, the year of its release, second only to STAR WARS. It would seem finally that Burt would have proved his point; would have been satisfied with his performance, not only as The Bandit but as the visionary who'd put SMOKEY together. However, this just wasn't the case. All the time he'd been making other people's pictures, he'd been complaining that he wanted the chance to do it his way, to make a Burt Reynolds picture. Yet, as the money came

rolling in, and it became clear that SMOKEY
was going to be a financial landmark, these were
Burt's sentiments: "My dilemma is that surrounding me now are not only very fine good ol'
boy scripts, but terrific directors who tell me,
'My last four pictures were artistic but not commercial successes. Hey, I want to make your
kind of picture,' and I'm saying to them, 'No,
you don't understand. I want to make your kind
of picture. I'm crazy about Billy Wilder. If I
had to pick three people to go away on a desert
island with he'd be one of them, but I think he'd
hate me as an actor," Burt told one reporter.
"Let me tell you something," he went on. I read
MAGIC and flipped. I thought it was fabulous.
But did anyone ask me if I was interested in
playing the part? Of course not. Maybe someone
even said, 'Oh, Reynolds, he doesn't do that kind
of thing.' But the truth is, I'd have killed to get
that part."

Fair enough. SMOKEY would put Burt at the
top of the Top Ten moneymakers, yet if he were
waiting for calls from other directors, specifically
the Coppollas, or the Scorceses, or the Formans,
the wait would be a long one. Where once he'd
felt boxed out, not he felt boxed in. Where his
rebellious nature had helped him create a billion
dollar southern movie industry, he seemed finally ready to come back into the fold, to take the
establishment by storm. He'd stuck his red neck
out and it was still in one piece.

nineteen

BURT was scheduled to go into production on SEMI-TOUGH as soon as SMOKEY was finished, but no sooner did he arrive back in Hollywood than he suffered a severe attack of chest pains, this time worse than he'd ever had before. At first he reached for the phone to call his friend Clint Eastwood, who'd half-convinced him that TM would make his anxiety attacks go away. After all, the doctors kept telling him he was all right, so it must be his state of mind.

Not being able to get Eastwood on the phone, Burt tried the TM center to find out what his mantra was. A woman on the other end of the line refused to give it to him. "How do I know you're Burt Reynolds?" she asked, finally giving him just a hint, that it had something to do with automobiles and happiness. Trying every possible combination of "Happy Fender," he chanted until he collapsed into a frenzy of hyperventilation. This time, Burt figured, he was definitely going to die. Reaching one last time for the phone, he called the emergency number, requesting an ambulance be sent for him immediately. Burt recounted what happened next, for

181

an interviewer: "Now, I'm on so many movie-star maps that everybody in Hollywood knows where my house is. But the ambulance couldn't find it. They passed it three times. Finally, I laid down in the street until they stopped for me."

He was taken to Cedars-Sinai Hospital, where a team of doctors worked over him in the emergency room, once again unable to find anything wrong. Finally, he was placed in a semi-private ward "for observation" with, as Burt later recalled "three old Jewish guys."

"I'm dying," he told one of them, who replied, "We're all dying. Do you want to play Gin Rummy?" What the hell, Burt took the deck and shuffled, spending the rest of the night playing cards, interrupted only once by a nurse asking for an autograph.

Released the next day with strict orders to take a total rest for at least two months, Burt found himself in a quandary. SEMI-TOUGH was scheduled to go into production immediately. Any postponement due to his illness would revive the bad health rumors and maybe create insurance problems. As it turned out, while Burt sat up in Bel-Air trying to figure out what to do, Michael Ritchie, the film's director, called Burt to tell him some bad news. There was trouble getting permission to use the Orange Bowl, Miami's football stadium, where some of SEMI-TOUGH's action was to be shot. At that point, Burt suggested a month-long break in shooting, until all problems could be worked out. Ritchie jumped at the idea. It was, as Burt would describe it, "a miracle."

He was scared. More than scared; petrified. There had been one too many visits to hospitals while feeling at death's edge, only to be told there was nothing wrong with him. He could doubt the doctors a lot quicker than he could his own feelings. So he did what he did whenever he felt scared: he went home to Jupiter.

Burt arrived in West Palm Beach the next day and checked into a hospital for a complete examination. The hospitals of West Palm Beach were a lot different than those of Beverly Hills. Here he just wasn't another crazy, pampered movie star with a crisis-causing blemish. Here he was king, every ache a cause for major concern. The doctors assured him if there was something wrong with him, they'd find out. And they did.

Exhausting all other possibilities, one doctor put Burt through a six-hour blood sugar test, and by doing so, finally discovered the cause of the palpitations, the sweats, the fatigue, and the hyperventilations. Burt was suffering from hypoglycemia, or chronic low blood sugar. With an excess of sugar in the blood, the pancreas produces insulin, resulting in a burst of "sugar" energy followed by fatigue, resulting in the body's further desire for more sugar. The cycle is relentless and the burden on the pancreas often leads to diabetes. In order to correct his hypoglycemia, Burt was put on a strict diet. He was required to give up all drinking and sweets. Smoking a joint was out because it would make him crave sweets, this last medical condition known as the "Hungry Horrors."

Burt was so relieved to find out that there was really something wrong with him and that he was going to live, he vowed never to take another drink; to take charge of his body, going on a campaign to restore himself to the superb condition he was in when he'd played college ball.

By the time he reported to the set of SEMI-TOUGH, a lot more than his diet had changed. For one thing, there was his relationship with Sally Field, who'd come to Florida to nurse Burt through his hospitalization. Giving up a chance to play Lois Lane in SUPERMAN to do so, she'd let Burt know that their relationship was going to be different than any he'd had in the past. She was a private person, and so would their relationship be. No weekly quotable quotes to the press. No public displays, rumors or innuendoes. She informed him she didn't intend to wait forever. Although she would like nothing better than to have Burt for a husband, the perfect "man's man," a fine father figure for her two young boys, if he were really serious, he'd have to get serious, really.

For Burt, Sally seemed perfect, although there were some problems he hadn't foreseen. Sure, he wanted children, but he wanted his own children, his own family. He wanted to experience fatherhood from the moment a man finds out his wife is pregnant, through that first look through the delivery room windows, the wet diapers, all of it. "Trust me," he told Sally, and he was convincing. If he was good enough to trust, in terms of her career, and he'd certainly proved that, he was good enough to trust about their future.

They both agreed they were a little too old to
"go steady." When the time came, Burt assured
Sally, he would make a decision; the right decision.

While SEMI-TOUGH was in production, GA-
TOR opened around the country to pleasant reviews and spectacular box-office. Universal Pictures, which had distributed SMOKEY AND
THE BANDIT, made Burt an offer of $2 mil-
lion just to agree to make a sequel, SMOKEY
AND THE BANDIT, PART II, with the rest of
the financial terms to be worked out later.
SMOKEY was Universal's top grossing movie in
1977 and had made multimillionaires out of
Burt and Hal Needham. Burt told the studio he
would do the sequel, when he was ready and
Needham was available. It must have made him
feel pretty terrific throwing the ball around the
Orange Bowl while Universal Studios was holding its breath back in Hollywood, waiting for a
nod of his head to start SMOKEY II. Jill Clayburgh was never quite sure why Burt was smiling
all the time; if it was the SMOKEY II deal, or
the fact that she'd reminded him on the first day
of shooting that he'd never "called her back," as
he promised, when she'd been one of the many
unknown actresses he'd dated after Dinah; one
of the nameless and faceless who now had quite
a name and what a face. From the first day on
the set, Burt and Jill had a great time filming
SEMI-TOUGH. Sally Field could tell you; she
was there for most of the shooting, standing on

the fifty yard line of Burt's life, watching every play old #22 made.

Just friends, just friends was what Burt and Chris Evert kept insisting to the press. Burt would joke later to Chris, as he would to other women he'd been "romantically linked" with that as long as they were guilty, they might as well commit the crime, his way of taking the edge off a situation that could become clumsy for whatever woman he happened to be seen with, photographed with, or actually dating. Denying his reputation as a "great lover," in that soft-spoken, smirking way he had of saying no but looking yes, Burt claimed that "ninety percent" of the women he was supposed to have been intimate with he "hardly knew at all."

That left quite a hefty ten percent. Just because he sent Chris Evert flowers every time she won a tournament; just because he flew to New York to watch her compete in a Madison Square Garden Tournament, and just because he was photographed with her at the time more than Sally, he assured everyone it didn't mean a thing. They'd met during the filming of SEMI-TOUGH, they both loved tennis, they were both from Florida, that was all there was to it.

It seemed, though, that he was testing the limits of his new "serious" relationship with Sally Field, to find out possibly just how far he could go. If he really didn't want any rumors of a relationship with Chris to be splashed across every newspaper in America, he could have arranged things so that Evert had a bit more privacy, especially since she was still licking the wounds from her celebrated break-up with Jimmy Conners, ripe-ready for a non-binding romantic involvement with America's favorite movie star.

In many ways, Burt with Sally, was reliving his relationship with Dinah Shore, inverting the roles so that now it was Sally who was the relative unknown and Burt the established, well-loved public figure. This time, it was Sally who was "privileged" to downshift and peel out into the fast lane. "Trust me," implied no matter what. The question remained, though, how much "No matter what" would Sally be willing to tolerate before it turned into "Enough's enough."

SEMI-TOUGH completed production late in 1977. No sooner had Burt shot his last scene than he took off for Atlanta, arriving just in time for the biggest event in that city since the 1939 premiere of GONE WITH THE WIND. Burt's Place, a million dollar bar/disco/restaurant, located in the famous Omni underground, was about to swing its doors open to the public. Designed as a major tourist attraction, Burt's Place was a gift to his hometown, meant to be the biggest, most glamorous restuarant in the world. Resembling a gigantic Hollywood movie studio, Burt's Place was a cavernous, multi-tiered extravaganza with rooms designed as movie sets from some of the most famous movies ever made. Here was an authentic trolley car room from STREETCAR NAMED DESIRE now converted to a sit-down bar complete with electronic New Orleans sound effects

piped in over the loudspeakers. Over there was
the entranceway to Hernando's Hideaway, from
THE PAJAMA GAME, complete with fifties
juke-box music. Still further yonder was Tara,
from GONE WITH THE WIND, and beyond
that, the western streets of HIGH NOON, next
door to the oriental paradise of TEAHOUSE OF
THE AUGUST MOON, followed, still further
on, by the creole atmosphere of SHOWBOAT's
expansive top-deck. Diners were able to choose
from such delicacies as Rhett Butler's Pleasure
Tempting Fried Chicken, with collard greens, of
course; or Cotton Blossom Gumbo and Home-
made corn muffins, from Burt's own secret recipe,
or, the ever-popular Jules Verne mouth watering
Shrimp Creole!

And that was just downstairs. Upstairs was
the Jock Bar, where drinks were served under
larger-than-life photos of Burt from THE
LONGEST YARD and the still-to-be-released
SEMI-TOUGH. Sitting in the Jock Bar with old
pal Dom DeLouise and Tammy Wynette, Burt
leaned back with his feet up and his smile wide
as he contemplated still another addition,
RICK'S ROOM, a room he could stroll through
in white tuxedo, scratching his lip Bogie-style,
while a tape recorder played the Marseillaise.
Here's looking at you, kid.

Opening night was truly memorable, with
Burt faring so much better than Margaret
Mitchell had on her big night, when the movie
made from her spectacular southern classic,
GONE WITH THE WIND, opened at the

Loew's Atlanta. On her way to the premiere, she was hit by a car and killed.

Coming on the heels of Burt's Place was the Burt Reynolds Dinner Theater. Within a rabbit's reach of Jupiter, Burt decided to open a huge theater where the biggest names in show business could come down and perform. It was almost as if he intended to repeat what he'd done with his movies when he'd taken them away from their established Hollywood studios, opening up the industry to film-making southern style. Now, with a $22 top, including a complete dinner and a terrific show, Burt seemed to be sending a message to that other town he felt he "didn't belong in." Perceiving the theatre as being in the stranglehold of a handful of Broadway producers—fat, cigar-chomping big shots who had a virtual lock on live dramatic talent—Burt sent about bringing the mountain to Mohammed. He would put the biggest stars into the most lavish productions imaginable. As 1977 came to a close, the first shovels sank into the Florida swampland, preparing the foundation for Burt's latest rebel shout. Theatre, y'all, southern style.

twenty

"I'D hate to see what they'd say if he made a movie with Lassie," Sally Field said when asked by a reporter about the constant rumors of Burt's romantic involvements. If she sounded a little defensive, it might have been because after SMOKEY, and playing nursemaid to Burt, she'd decided to do a picture independently, without any help or advice from Burt. HEROES, a post-Vietnam comedy co-starring Henry Winkler, TV's Fonzie, was as much a flop at the box office as SMOKEY had been a hit. Burt could have told her so, if only she'd asked. Even with the strength of an emmy behind her, HEROES proved that without Burt, she wasn't about to rewrite the box-office records. HEROES sent Sally running back into Burt's cinematic arms, where he immediately signed her up to co-star with him in his latest movie, THE END, a comedy he was going to produce about suicide. Trust me.

Hollywood couldn't ignore Burt's achievements, even if it wasn't quite ready to give him its coveted academy award. However, in 1978,

Burt was the number one box-office star in America; he deserved something. Just as he was ready to begin production on THE END, he was notified that the Hollywood Chamber of Commerce had elected to place his "Star" on Hollywood Boulevard. That March, Burt became the 1,-695th Hollywood personality to be honored in the legendary Walk of Fame. Burt's "Star" was placed at 6838 Hollywood Boulevard, between Jan Sterling and Pee Wee Hunt. It was a pleasant affair, with the venerable Monty Hall making the presentation, and various Hollywood Chamber of Commerce luminaries there to meet and greet, and the requisite crowd of fans and curious onlookers. This made sense to Burt. The boulevard was like the Hollywood movie industry, falling apart. Okay, they were giving him a slab of sidewalk cement; using his name to add a little polish to the heavily tarnished "Boulevard of Dreams." It was recognition of a sort, but it wasn't really. It would never be enough until the envelope was opened, the name announced, the trot up the steps and the gold-plated statue. That was when you arrived in this town; when no one walked over you. Smiling into the camera while his street-star was unveiled, Burt's real focus was in the direction of his latest film, the one he was itching to start production on.

THE END was a strange choice of films. SEMI-TOUGH was a box-office smash, the first "establishment" movie he'd made since the disastrous NICKLEODEON. Coming on the heels of GATOR, and of course, SMOKEY, Burt

was now in a position to pick and choose anything he wanted to do. Universal was still holding its breath for SMOKEY II. As Billy Clyde
Puckett, Burt had come closer than ever to combining the image of the new southern hero with
that of the old Hollywood star. What made
SEMI-TOUGH so successful was its upbeat
chemistry combining the smoke of the football
action with the exhaust from a Trans-Am. Jill
Clayburgh's thighs didn't hurt either. The next
logical career step for Burt would have been a
further marriage of Hollywood and the South,
SMOKEY II, for instance, with a little less grit
and a little more polish. Instead, Burt chose a
depressing "comedy" about a man who discovers
he's dying of an incurable disease and decides to
kill himself.

In the words of someone closely connected
with the making of THE END, the reason Burt
chose to make this film was obvious. In spite of
his success; all the money, recognition, acceptance and women, "he was depressed as hell.
That's why he was attracted to THE END in
the first place." At a press conference, Burt said
he got the idea for the film during his stay at
Cedars-Sinai hospital, playing cards with the old
guys in his room. Not so, according to the writer
of the picture, Jerry Belson, who claims his
script had made the rounds for years, with no
studio willing to come within twenty yards of it
until Burt decided he wanted to film it. Even
then, Burt had to agree to half his normal salary
and a cut in percentage money to get the film
made. And, in order to get approval to direct, he

had to agree to star in it as well. Even though publicly Burt was telling reporters he'd love to be able to direct a movie he didn't have to be in, insiders knew he was "dying" to play Sonny Lawson, the man without a future.

But why was Burt so depressed? As one friend put it, THE END came at a turning point in Burt's life, as well as his career. The regulation of his hypoglycemia hadn't totally convinced him he was in as good shape as his doctors insisted. He was in his forties now, and although he insisted that a leading man's best years on the screen were between thirty-five and fifty, the truth of the matter was that the lines on his forehead were deeper than any in Shakespeare's most profound plays. His days as the number one good ol' boy were obviously limited.

THE END was Burt's self-indulgence taken to the extreme and reflected as much at the box office where it was a relative loser, although any film that grosses $40 million should never be confused with HEAVEN'S GATE. It was a loser only in terms of Burt's other films which hovered around the hundred million mark or better. His undistinguished performance in THE END, coupled with his sluggish, lingering direction projected anything but humor on the screen. After appearing lean and hard in SEMI-TOUGH, Burt now appeared in the movie as a frumpy, middle-aged moral coward, afraid of his own shadow, surrounded by humorless caricatures of crazies like Carl Reiner and Dom DeLouise instead of the Dallas backfield. In fact, the only bright moment in the film was Sally Field as

Sonny's young and beautiful girl-friend who
tries, unsuccessfully, to nurse him back to
health. Made by anyone else, THE END would
have been a financial disaster. Starring Burt
Reynolds, it was a qualified success. However,
there was no beating around the bush. He was
disappointed by the film's box-office, taking its
rejection by the public personally. Throwing up
his hands, he decided it was time to take a break,
to get off the cinematic carousel. Next stop, The
Burt Reynolds Theatre.

The premiere attraction at The Burt Reynolds
Theatre was MR. ROBERTS, the first play that
Burt had appeared in on Broadway some twenty
years earlier, followed by THE RAINMAKER,
the play he'd done in Chicago to record-breaking
grosses shortly after the COSMO centerfold. It
was almost as if he were re-creating his past, returning to his youth via the stage, instead of
visualizing his "end" on the screen. He starred in
THE RAINMAKER again, as well as directing
the production, with Sally co-starring. The show
was a smash, with Burt dedicating the entire
production to his mother, whose picture adorned
the play's program. There was only one problem.
No one realized at the time that although Burt's
name appeared everywhere on the program, the
playwright's name, Thornton Wilder, had been
inadvertently left off.

Between shows, Burt took to making personal
appearances, utilizing the one-liner writing tal-
ents of Jerry Belson, after dinner on the dias or
with Johnny on "Tonight." At a personal ap-

pearance at the NATO conference in New York (NATO as in National Association of Theatre Owners, not the other one) Burt addressed the convention of theatre owners who were, at the time, somewhat disgruntled at having to buy pictures for their theatres without being able to see them in advance, a practice in the industry known as "blind-bidding." Burt, of course, was one of the three most popular stars at the convention. Along with Jane Fonda and Warren Beatty, he was one of the few stars whose name on the marquee literally guaranteed a hit at the box office. While sympathizing with the theatre owners, Burt was a producer now, and his appearance was as much a gesture of fence-mending as it was gratitude. Predictably, his off-the-cuff approach, coupled with his clever comments, won the nervous audience over to his side. "NATO and I have a common goal—for Burt Reynolds movies to make millions. I want you to remember when I make millions, you'll make hundreds . . . and I hate blind-bidding, because if it didn't exist, AT LONG LAST LOVE would never have been released." The audience roared.

Burt could be a real crowd-pleaser when he wanted to, such as when the city of Atlanta, showing its appreciation for all that Burt had done for it, threw a black-tie roast in his honor. Taking her cue from Burt's self-effacing brand of humor, Sally Field, one of the invited speakers, went to the mike on the dias, leaning in as if to share a secret with the audience, and said, "You look like a crowd I can trust. The truth is, the

man's a sex maniac. The hotel installed a take-
a-number machine outside his room. I got number eighty-eight but the line moves fast."
Turning to Burt, she added, "And do I have to
dress up like a fireman?" The place rocked with
laughter. Burt, approaching the microphone,
never missed a beat as he quietly and steadily informed the audience that, "Sally and I have had
this kind of wonderful relationship for the past
year. You were privileged tonight to see it end."

If he were a clap of laughing thunder in public, in private there were still some things on his
mind. As popular as he was, he continued to
seem pre-occupied by actors who got the recognition he felt he should be getting. Jack Nicholson, in particular, continued to plague Burt's
consciousness. Originally scheduled to make
STORM WARNING, a big-budget Hollywood
feature co-starring Robert Shaw, Burt told producer Peter Guber he would make the film under one condition. "How much is Nicholson
getting for THE SHINING?" he wanted to
know. When told that the figure was $3.2 mil-
lion, Burt insisted he get $3.5 million, or it was
no go.

It was no go.

Burt, more bitter than disappointed, began
making more and more reference to "The Big
Three"—Nicholson, Dustin Hoffman, whose
success Burt couldn't make heads nor tails of,
and, the critics' darling who could do no wrong,
Robert DeNiro. Hailed as the "new Marlon
Brando," a tag that must have particularly
irked Burt, DeNiro came to the movies from a

successful New York stage career, and also re-
tained his Italian street-smart bravado in film after film warmly accepted by the same critics who
rejected Burt's good ol' boy as so much chick-pea
soup. It didn't seem to bother anybody that
Burt's "Bandit" was far closer to his own reality
than DeNiro's street-hoodlum was to his. De-
Niro, in fact, was from an elite background,
his father one of the legitimate avant-garde artists connected in New York's plushy gallery set,
making the young DeNiro's ethnic working-class
screen heroes even more remarkable. What must
have angered Burt, though, was that DeNiro
copped an academy award for playing Marlon
Brando as a young man in THE GODFATHER,
PART II (and would later pick up a second Oscar for his portrayal of boxer-turned-animal in
RAGING BULL) while Burt, for all his box-
office success and adulation down south, never
even got nominated for an academy award. It
didn't seem to matter to anyone that Burt's
films were commercially more successful than
DeNiro's. DeNiro's films averaged $20 million
in grosses, while Burt's came in at around $100
million per. What did matter, apparently, was
that although DeNiro's movies were big box-office in only two cities, those two cities were New
York and Los Angeles, where Burt's pictures traditionally did their poorest. Burt, commenting
in *Playboy* on DeNiro and Hoffman: "My jeal-
ousy isn't directed at them, it's directed toward
the Coppolas and other directors who won't give
me a shot because I'm a movie star. . . . When
was the last time you heard someone say,

'Let's go see DeNiro?' In New York, maybe, but in Iowa, or Alabama . . . I would like to see me doing THE DEER HUNTER or RAGING BULL, and I'd like to see him play Billy Clyde Puckett in SEMI-TOUGH. I would like to play LENNY and see Hoffman do W.W. AND THE DIXIE DANCEKINGS. . . . I think I'd be able to do pictures *they've* done better than they could do pictures *I've* done." Burt had a special thing against Coppola. If there was one role he'd wanted to play, it was that of Sonny Corleone, and he hadn't even been able to get Coppola to return his calls. At least one Hollywood director saw things differently. Robert Aldrich, while sympathetic, explained it this way: "He's probably right in not being recognized as being as good an actor as he is. I think he's upset with the Hollywood community because they never nominate him. He's right to a point. Making movies is like football. If the quarterback drops back to pass, you have to go out for the catch. In other words, if he wants to go out and make his type of movies, you can't expect somebody to evaluate them like they would a Marty Scorcese picture. It's not the same ten yards, and that upsets him I suspect."

There was no doubt about it. Burt was checking his watch and sensing his time was passing. So, turning his back on Hollywood once again, he took Hal Needham and Sally down to Mobile, Alabama to make yet another southern movie.

HOOPER was southern good ol' boy, but with a difference. Whereas Burt had always been the ultimate guy without a care in the world, HOOPER told the tale of a stuntman too old to perform his tricks anymore. Burt, indeed, looked old as he huffed and puffed his way through the stunts he insisted on doing himself. Like an aging rock star refusing to look in the mirror, Burt continued to surround himself with familiar faces and an entourage of yes-men. If Burt's petulance and fears of aging were making things difficult for Sally on the set, the crazy letters she was receiving in the mail every day from angry, obviously jealous women weren't helping. "You stink so much that not even Burt can help you. . . . Get out of his life," was one of the gentler notes she received. As soon as HOOPER was finished. Burt told Universal it was time to make SMOKEY II.

Burt decided to take a vacation with Sally before starting SMOKEY II, which was having script problems, going through several writers and titles, including SMOKEY AND THE BANDIT HAVE A BABY. Rejecting all scripts, Burt finally decided on putting the writing into the hands of the capable Jerry Belson, while he and Sally went off to Maui for some well-earned R and R.

On Maui, Burt and Sally ran into a couple of his old pals, actor Jim Nabors and football player Russ Francis. It was like a shot in the arm for Burt, who began churning up his engine of energy, playing around with the boys during the day, grabbing Sally by the arm and hitting the beaches at night. Nabors, meanwhile, was spouting off to Burt about how great Hawaii was, the last American frontier, with plenty of cheap land available for investment purposes. As if to impress Burt, Nabors took him, Sally, and Francis to a steep cliff, 150 sheer feet above the rocky blue-green waters of the Pacific. It was as if the rest of the mountainside had been cleaved by a giant axe, leaving this little peak high above the foamy rush of sea. Suddenly, Burt turned to Francis and challenged him to a "jump." Before Francis could respond, Burt thrust his arms in front of him and dove head first into the swirling Pacific. A second later, Francis followed. Horrified, Sally and Nabors immediately left the cliff to search the shores for the two men, already fearing the worst.

They found them a half-mile downstream, on the beach, flat on their backs. Burt, smiling, told Sally as matter-of-factly as if he were asking her to pass the suntan lotion that he would be dead now if Russ ol' buddy hadn't pulled him to the shore.

There was still more bizarre behavior from Burt. Cruising with Sally aboard a luxury liner on the Caribbean, Burt, without warning, dove over the side, only to be hauled back on board seconds later by an efficient, if greatly puzzled crew. Suffering nothing worse than a prick from a tangy blowfish, he seemed elated at pulling off this latest stunt, gushing to Sally about how much fun it had been.

He may have been having a ball risking death to prove he was still alive, but to Sally, it was no fun. What had begun as a no-strings-attached commitment to "trust" was rapidly turning into an endless cycle of movies, money, and vacations, an endless repetition of fun and games with Burt hardly ever mentioning marriage anymore. Needless to say, the newspapers, hungry for material on their favorite celebrity, seemed to be speculating as much on the possibility of Burt's marriage to Sally as on the situation in the Middle East. The more Sally hinted at commitment, though, the more Burt took to diving off cliffs and ships. At one point, she built on an extra addition to her home, so he could be close to her kids. Burt, however, preferred Bel-Air to the Valley, content to let Sally stay forever on her side of the mountain, while he lived it up in bachelor splendor with Hal Needham, the two oldest teenagers in Hollywood. By the time SMOKEY II began shooting, Burt had resuscitated his movie schedule so that he would make, without taking a day off, CANNONBALL RUN, ROUGH CUT, and THE BEST LITTLE WHOREHOUSE IN TEXAS, taking him well into 1980 without a break. Sally could trust Burt into oblivion.

He was ready to start SMOKEY II, but the script still wasn't ready for him. While the last problems were being sorted out, Burt read James Brooks' screenplay for STARTING OVER and was convinced that this film could be the one to finally do it, to give him a real shot at finally winning an Oscar. With Alan Pakula directing, this solid, urbane, sophisticated comedy seemed the perfect cure for Burt's real or imagined

middle-age blues; the story of a man coming to
terms with his past as he faces an uncertain future. For Burt, STARTING OVER would be
just that, his reconciliation with establishment
movie-making Hollywood and elitist New York.

twenty-one

As Phil Potter, Burt was cast totally against type. Potter is a passive, upper-middle-class New York school teacher married to a wacky, sexy pop songwriter in a marriage crumbling almost before the opening credits are finished. Separating from his wife, Potter moves to Boston to be near his psychologist brother and meets a hyper-feminist Jill Clayburgh, with whom he falls unhappily ever-after in love, only to have his ex (Candy Bergen) show up the day he and Clayburgh decide to move in together. Seduced by Bergen, Potter moves back to New York, realizes he really loves Clayburgh, returns to Boston, proposes to, and finally gets Jill. The only car Burt drives in the film is a Volkswagen, which he loses control of during a snowstorm. Burt's Phil Potter is post-divorce impotent, passive, and shy to the point of pain. Even his toupee was a departure; instead of the rugged, curly longish hair Burt and his audience were so used to, Potter's was a close-cropped, Ivy League razor-cut, serving to emphasize the lines in Burt's face rather than compete with them for attention.

Although the film was a commercial and criti-

cal success, it hadn't been all that easy for
Burt to get the part. Although he'd gotten in
touch with director Alan Pakula as soon as he'd
put the screenplay down, Pakula understandably
didn't have Burt at the top of his most wanted
list. Pakula was looking to go with Robert Redford or Dustin Hoffman. So intent was Burt on
playing Phil Potter that he turned down an offer
from Neil Simon to play opposite Marsha
Mason in CHAPTER TWO, the role eventually
going to James Caan.

Sally, meanwhile, plunged herself into BE-
YOND THE POSEIDON ADVENTURE on
Burt's advice. After all, she might have some fun
doing POSEIDON while he was busy with
STARTING OVER. For her part, she was interested in buying properties for future develop-
ment, specifically heavyweight novels like
SOPHIE'S CHOICE. No way, Burt told her.
Those were exactly the wrong types of projects
for her to be involved in. Better to buy pulpy
adventure stories like SPHINX; sure-fire
money-makers. Sally, seeing the logic in Burt's
arguments, put off buying the rights to SO-
PHIE'S CHOICE. Although POSEIDON was
shot before NORMA RAE, it wasn't released
until after Sally won her Oscar for her portrayal
of the rebellious union leader. When the silly sea
adventure flopped, failing to cash in on the fortune the original POSEIDON ADVENTURE
had made, Burt openly admitted he'd given Sally
bad advice, but with the best of intentions. Burt
always enjoyed playing Svengali, turning car
crashes into the box-office gold, being the prince

to Sally's frog. Once discovered, though, she'd quickly become the new girl in town, echoing the days when Burt was the background to Judy Carne's very noticeable foreground. If things had been touch-and-go before Burt went into STARTING OVER, when he was gently urging Sally to go out and make some movies, they started to come apart when Sally flew unexpectedly to New York, to be with Burt for the filming of some scenes for STARTING OVER, and found him with Candy, in Sally's own words, "with his hand in the cookie jar." She was furious. It was one thing to read about Burt's endless exploits in the newspapers and to have them fluffed off by him as so much nonsense; it was quite another to nail him in the act. In order to cool things out, Burt gave Sally a $40,000 mink coat, and sweetened Candy with a $15,-000 bracelet. All in all, it was an expensive fling.

However, things collapsed completely when Sally, after completing POSEIDON ADVENTURE II, accepted the title role in NORMA RAE, and was nominated for an Academy Award.

Later on, Burt would take much pride in relating to friends how he'd read the NORMA RAE script and predicted Sally would win an Oscar by turning to her and saying, "the envelope, please." What he hadn't counted on was NORMA RAE and STARTING OVER both being nominated for a wealth of Oscars. It seemed that everyone connected with the two pictures was up for an Academy Award. Every-

one, that is, except Burt, who was conspicuously
left out of the Best Actor category for his role in
STARTING OVER. Worse, Sally was compet-
ing for the Oscar with Marsha Mason, for her
portrayal of herself in the film Burt turned
down, CHAPTER TWO. The main buzz on "Oscar Night" was how Burt would react if Sally
won the big one. The real surprise came, though,
when Sally, arriving at the Dorothy Chandler
Pavillion, stepped out of her limousine escorted
by David Steinberg, a close friend, instead of
Burt, who was nowhere in sight. He didn't show
up at all that night, sending nuclear power into
the exploding rumors that the already unstable
relationship between him and Sally was blown
apart by the Oscars.

Why wasn't Burt there with Sally? "When
you send somebody a note saying you'd be glad
to go with them and they don't even answer, it's
fairly obvious they're not interested." Being
snubbed by Sally, though, was one thing. Getting
the brush by the Academy was something else
again. Burt's failure to receive a nomination for
Best Actor in STARTING OVER probably had
a lot more to do with his not showing up than
anything else. As if to add insult to injury, the
Academy had invited Burt to be one of its
presenters; always a bridesmaid, never an Oscar.
With both Jill Clayburgh and Candy Bergen
nominated for STARTING OVER, this last gesture by the Academy was just too much for
Burt.

His disappointment was not hard to understand. As undisputed king of the southern

movies, he'd made a giant gesture to establishment Hollywood, a town that always rewarded its repenters. For example, when Humphrey Bogart was squiring Mary Astor around town, there was talk that Warner Brothers was on the verge of dropping him for carrying on with the notorious "diary lady" whose prolific sex life became a worldwide front-page scandal during her divorce. However, once the celluloid tough-guy settled down to serious matters, like marrying Lauren Bacall and letting his beard grow scruffy for THE AFRICAN QUEEN, Oscar came his way. Cary Grant, through dozens of unforgettable performances had never gotten the golden nod until he, too, went scruffy for the otherwise ordinary FATHER GOOSE, resulting in an Oscar nomination. Even the legendary Duke, passed over for forty years by the Academy, in spite of nerve-cracking performances in dozens of American classic motion pictures, had to don an eyepatch and go scruffy, before he was to collect his Oscar for TRUE GRIT. After making a career out of playing scruffy action-adventure Southern heroes, Burt, in STARTING OVER, had made his attempt to "go establishment," Hollywood-style, putting on a suit and tie and playing totally against type. As he put it, bitterly, after being passed over by the Academy, "Until I get a tracheotomy or go to work for a perfume company, I'll never be nominated. I know if word got around I only had a year to live, I'd get nominated."

Others in Hollywood who knew Burt saw it a little differently. Robert Aldrich, commenting on

Burt's failure to receive a nomination for
STARTING OVER, pointed out that if he
"didn't want to be tagged as making only Burt
Reynolds movies, he has to make movies that
aren't Burt Reynolds movies, like STARTING
OVER. What happened, though, was that halfway through the movie he fell back into that
Burt Reynolds stuff that he's so appealing at.
That was not that character. So maybe he did
himself a disservice. How come everyone got
nominated for that picture but him? I think
what happened is that he strayed off that character. He wanted the audience to love him, but he
didn't want to be a lousy guy."

By the time SMOKEY AND THE BANDIT
II went into production, the word on the set was
not to hang around if Sally and Burt were in the
same scene; things could get out of hand. They
were hardly speaking to each other now. No
amount of editing in the world could make Sally
look into Burt's eyes during SMOKEY II, a fact
that gave the film an odd, cold quality. While
SMOKEY II broke all box-office records the first
weeks it played, settling down to a long and
healthy run (though not racking up nearly as
much as the original SMOKEY), it seemed clear
it would be the last go-around for SMOKEY,
and the last time Burt would work together with
Sally in a movie.

Just before he left for England to star in
ROUGH CUT, he consented to an interview
with Barbara Walters on "The Today Show."

What he didn't know was that his segments were going to be intercut with others made with Sally. "I had no idea they were going to do that," Burt told one interviewer later. "I was furious, I felt totally manipulated. The next thing I knew, their crew ran out of the house, jumped in a car and flew to Alabama where she was making a picture (BACK ROADS). They not only played her what I said, they filmed her watching it. It sure didn't help our relationship. I'm not a John Derek type, but I felt there were things I could tell her, in terms of fame . . . I had been there and I thought, if I can't help her any other way, this is one area I could help her in." Sally saw things a little differently: "There is no way you can know why you won an award like the Oscar. You can't set out to win one." Insisting, though, that their relationship was fine, she was nevertheless moved when she heard Burt say, on that same "Today" show, that "I love her very, very much. I was actually totally overjoyed about her winning the award regardless of what you read in the press." So, according to Burt, he enjoyed playing Pygmalion, even when Galatea stole his thunder. As if to prove his point, he made sure that when Sally woke up one morning in front of her house she'd find a shiny black Trans-Am, à la The Bandit's, with the license plates BRTS GRL there for the world to see. Some guys like to send notes, or boxes of candy, or flowers. Burt's thing was cars.

While Sally stayed home with the kids and the Trans-Am, Burt was busy shifting gears in Lon-

don, playing with Lesley Ann Down in David
Merrick's ROUGH CUT. The British Press
which loves to scream Hollywood scandal on its
front pages, made a real mess of things describing in detail the alleged romance between Burt
and Down. If Burt and Down dominated the
front pages of the tabloids, David Niven all but
stole the film from them, showing Burt how
suavity was supposed to be played, sending Burt
into a frenzy of I-Miss-America. He returned
just in time to receive the news that he had made
it to the top of the box-office attractions again in
1979, his second year in a row, and if the returns from the just-released CANNONBALL
RUN were any indication, he'd be on top again
in 1980.

It was funny. CANNONBALL RUN was
little more than a private joke for Hal Needham
and Burt, getting a gang of their pals together
and throwing the film in the can on the heels of
SMOKEY II. CANNONBALL RUN, the story
of a cross-country car race without rules, was
little more than an excuse to waste gas, a fantasy
all America seemed ready to indulge. The $5
million Burt received for *Cannonball Run*, quite
obviously added to his fun. The film, filled
with an assortment of international stars, including Dean Martin, Roger Moore, Dom DeLouise,
and Sammy Davis, was reminiscent of the kind
of films Frank Sinatra used to make when, between Vegas gigs, he'd want to clown around
with the "rat pack" for pay. CANNONBALL
RUN, thrown together in almost no time,
proved to be box-office gold, easily out-grossing

SMOKEY II. The studios were clamoring for more product from Burt, but he told them they'd have to be a little patient. His first stop, back in America, was the Burt Reynolds Theatre.

In many ways, Burt's theatre was his greatest source of pleasure, where no studio heads could tell him what he should or shouldn't be doing, no agents, no PR gorillas, no jaded starlets or overblown prima donnas making demands. Here he called the shots, inviting talented friends and colleagues in to do shows. Even Judy Carne, out of work and in trouble with the law because of her involvement with drugs, was given a chance to do some no-frills acting at Burt's Florida theatre. Joanne Woodward was invited to come down as well.

The "Citrus Circuit" had always been a Broadway joke until Burt's Theatre proved it could be a big money-maker. Burt used his theatre to develop the skill he was most interested in now—directing. With two films under his belt, GATOR and THE END, Burt was planning to put an end to his days as the oldest living good ol' boy to get behind the camera to direct, where he felt he belonged.

One of Burt's greatest pleasures in connection with his theatre was the apprentice program he'd set up in connection with Florida State University's theatre program and other universities and colleges nearby. Every year, twenty students were chosen out of hundreds that applied, to be apprentices in a work-study program. The students came under Burt's personal direction.

He wanted to "save them" from falling into the traps that he'd experienced in his early days, when he couldn't find anyone in the world who would take him seriously. It was Burt's way of giving back, and it wasn't just talk and tokenism. Along with the work-study program, Burt donated $600,000 to FSU to set up an endowed theatre professorship in his honor. Some saw this return to Florida as Burt's way of trying to retrieve the past, to relive his own youth through the lives of the fresh-faced and eager young kids so ready to work deep into the night building sets and painting scenery. Others saw it as his attempt to break the endless real-life boy-meets-girl, boy-gets-girl-boy-loses-girl relationship with Sally, who kept insisting that her idea of the perfect husband was a guy she could rely on, someone who could put some stability into her emotional life. Why would she want to marry a guy who treated her the way Burt Reynolds treated women?

The truth was, by 1981, they both knew it was over, but they were both afraid to admit it.

twenty-two

"WHEN a man breaks up with a woman, especially when the man is me, there's a tendency to assume it was my idea. I think everyone should give Sally credit for being stronger than people think she is. I'm sure the relationship would still be going on if she hadn't had the strength to say, 'Shape up or ship out.' I did want to shape up . . . and I still do. I'm just not sure I want to do it on demand." There was no doubt about it, by 1981 the stormy relationship between Burt and Sally was as flat as last year's champagne. Just not able to bring himself to the altar, he reluctantly pulled back, letting Sally go.

If there was any solace to be had, it came from the fact that for the third year in a row he made it to the top of the box-office list of top-grossing stars. Only one other person had pulled off the feat three years running, Doris Day, 1962-1964. Nicholson's name was not even near the Top Ten. Nor was DeNiro's, nor Pacino's, nor Woody Allen's. 1980 was all Reynolds-wrapped, Oscar or no Oscar. He was the peo-

ple's champion, and no one could take that
away from him.

As such, there was nothing that was beyond
him. Having met and become friendly with
David Steinberg while both were guests on "The
Tonight Show," Burt was taken with the young
comic's urbane wittiness, and before long the
two were huddling together, forming an independent production company to make movies they
would produce, direct, and star in. Steinberg had
long wanted a movie career in the Woody Allen
mold. Burt felt a chemistry between himself and
Steinberg, and it didn't hurt at all that Steinberg's wife and Sally were very close friends. In
fact, if Burt were looking for a way to patch
things up with Sally, what better way than to
put a film package together in which he, Steinberg, and Sally could all participate.

Burt found PATERNITY, the story of a man
who wants to have a baby, but doesn't want to
get married. Rich, successful, a ladies' man,
Buddy Evans searches in vain for the right
"mother," finally settling on Maggie, a waitress
putting herself through Juilliard, who takes on
the job for $50,000. Of course, Burt falls in love
with Maggie, and the three—Burt, Maggie, and
the one on the way—live happily ever after. So
close was Burt to this script that he used his
former nickname, Buddy, for his character, and
up until the last possible moment was certain
that Sally would play Maggie.

As soon as word leaked that Burt was looking to make another movie with Sally, rumors of
an impending marriage proposal buzzed through

Hollywood again. Even Sally wasn't sure what the status of their relationship was, except that she hoped it wasn't over. How could it be if Burt still wanted her to be in his movies, she reasoned. Yet, at the last moment, for whatever reason, Burt had a change of heart and cast Beverly D'Angelo, a relative unknown, as Maggie.

Tensions increased between Burt and David Steinberg, both on and off the set. Word from one crew member was that by the time PATERNITY finished shooting, the two were hardly speaking to each other. Part of the reason had to be Burt's sense of movie-making perfection. The first day of shooting on the set of THE END, Burt had Jerry Belson, the screenwriter, thrown off the set for making a suggestion about how a scene should be shot. Now, with two films under his directing Garrison Belt, Burt seemed to be at loggerheads with Steinberg, whose comic technique seemed a trifle too sweet for the swaggering Reynolds style. Also, the fact that Burt and Sally were once again on the outs may have brought some unnecessary pressure from Steinberg. When PATERNITY failed to reunite Burt and Sally, Steinberg's disappointment was hard for him to conceal.

With off-screen tensions intruding on PATERNITY, not only from Burt's off-again off-again romance with Sally, but also from impending shutdowns due to the actor's strike, the film never realized its comic potential and ultimately was not as successful at the box office as Burt's other big pictures. Shortly after its release, Burt and Steinberg announced the dissolution of their

joint production company. The feeling from
those close to the two was that Burt's split from
Sally caused his split from Steinberg.

Burt returned to Hollywood early in 1981
to complete the trouble-plagued filming of the
hit Broadway musical THE BEST LITTLE
WHOREHOUSE IN .TEXAS. Burt, who had
originally turned down the project, finally told
its producers the only way he would make the
film was if Dolly Parton would play opposite
him. Parton, meanwhile, told the producers she'd
make the film only if Burt Reynolds were in it.
Finding themselves in a most enviable position,
the producers of WHOREHOUSE were able,
without too much trouble, to negotiate the
dream-cast for what they believed would be the
can't-miss musical of the decade. However, there
were problems almost from the start. Both Burt
and Dolly were unsatisfied with the script and
demanded continual rewrites. The actor's strike
which had interfered with the filming of PA-
TERNITY, caused Dolly Parton to revise her
concert schedule, making it more difficult than
ever to clear enough time to devote to the filming of the picture. Tommy Tune, originally
signed to direct, left the production over "artistic differences," which insiders claim was his in-
ability to get along with Burt. Further, Parton
insisted she be allowed to write her own songs,
while Burt required the romantic angle between
the sheriff and Dolly, the mistress of the
"house," be expanded. The filming, and non-film-
ing dragged on for months, through the end of

the long strike, through the long winter months, until Burt, somewhat perturbed at how things were going, came across a script which he wanted to star in and direct as soon as possible. SHARKY'S MACHINE excited Burt as no picture had for a long, long time. The story of a detective in Atlanta, Georgia's elite "Prince" squad, narcotics, is on the trail of a big-time dealer. In the course of apprehending him, a gunfight ensues and Sharky involves an innocent busdriver in the battle, causing him to be severely wounded. As a result, Sharky is demoted to the vice squad, the bottom of the police barrel.

It's on the vice squad that Sharky puts together his "machine," made up of the dregs of the department—the has-beens and the never-weres—to expose organized crime involvement at the highest state level, leading straight to the governor's mansion. The connection between organized crime and the governor is made through Sharky's stumbling upon the governor's mistress, a pretty, husky-voiced prostitute, Dominoe, played by newcomer Rachel Ward. In the process of "surveillance" of Dominoe's apartment, in the hopes of catching her "in action," Sharky becomes fascinated with her comings and goings, and during the course of the movie comes face to face with her "mentor," played by the venerable Vittorio Gassman. Along the way, Sharky falls in love with Dominoe and takes her away to his private home-away-from-home, the house he grew up in, now abandoned, vacant ex-

cept for his occasional visits; not unlike Superman's fortress of solitude.

Why was SHARKY'S MACHINE so ap-
pealing to Burt? Because he saw the film's police
precinct as a metaphor for the film industry; his
desire to be the "Prince" of Hollywood and New
York, the same as Sharky's desire to be one of
Atlanta's elite. However, because of his rebellious attitude, Sharky is forced to do vice work,
a nice parallel for the endless action and adventure stunt films Burt did for so many years. Further, Burt's anger at Coppola and envy for
DeNiro and Pacino seem personified by Gassman's greasy, capo de capa, boss of bosses—the
enemy, the unattainable and untouchable power
heads in control of movies, or prostitution, both
areas of make-believe.

Finally, though, there is Sharky's fascination
with Dominoe. For long periods of the movie we
view the gorgeous hooker as Sharky does,
through various camera lenses, much in the way
a director would frame his shots. We watch
Dominoe "act out" her prostitute games for her
clients, and we actually see the process of idol-
ization and fantasy dissolve into real-life, as
Sharky somehow manages to inject himself into
Dominoe's real/fantasy world, "playing a role"
in order to "save" her, not unlike the way he'd
"rescued" Sally Field from her aborted acting
career. Almost every aspect of SHARKY reflects
some aspect of Burt's real life, down to his new,
short-haired receding toupee. Chunkier than in
past films, with ever deeper lines in his face,

Sharky/Burt was a genuine revelation. Asked why he made the film, which he dubbed, DIRTY HARRY GOES TO ATLANTA, Burt facetiously replied that he was a little "angry" with Clint for turning away from hard-line adventure to make films like ANY WHICH WAY BUT LOOSE, strictly Burt's territory, and he therefore had a right to make Dirty Harry movies. Actually, though, SHARKY'S MACHINE was a very personal statement for Burt, much closer to the real drama of his life than the egoistic PATERNITY. Here, with SHARKY, was Burt dealing with his fears of growing older, still bucking the system while wanting desperately to be a part of it. Here was a chance to pull all the stops out, to combine action with pathos, drama with humor, as opposed to stunts-as-comedy.

Once again, Burt had plucked a virtually unknown beauty, Rachel Ward, an English model previously linked romantically with David Kennedy, the late Senator Robert Kennedy's son, to be his co-star. Rumors of their romantic involvement began even before Burt cast her in the film, a mere five days before shooting began. There was some talk before then that Burt was thinking of using Sally to play Dominoe. In fact, when it was officially confirmed that Rachel Ward was to play the part, Sally declared it was the "last straw," and moved out of her own house in Hollywood, disgusted with herself, with Burt, and with the whole Hollywood scene. She even informed him he was not to be in touch with her children; his influence was no longer wanted, his presence no longer required. As she explained to one newspaper, "If I ever get married again, it'll be a guy who can fix the toilet."

If Burt was affected by his break-up with Sally, he didn't show it. In fact, he seemed so absorbed by SHARKY'S MACHINE he barely had time to acknowledge the awards and accolades that were being heaped on him, one coming on the heels of another. In January of 1981, Burt was awarded an honorary Doctor of Humane Letters from Florida State University, an award that so moved him to took time out from his schedule to personally appear to accept the honor. Later, he was given an official Friar's Roast, an honor bestowed on only the industry's most revered stars. It was New York extending its own olive branch, and Burt was there with bells on to accept. Held at the Waldorf-Astoria Grand Ballroom, 1,200 of the biggest names in entertainment turned out, to the tune of $175-to-$225 a plate to pay homage to The Man. Hosting the affair, fittingly, was Johnny Carson, "The Tonight Show's" own "prince," there to pat his buddy on the back for a job well done. It was quite a high night. The jokes came fast and furious. Noting Governor's Carey's absence, Carson said he was busy taking a recount of his wife's ex-husbands. Topping off the entire evening, though, was none other than Dinah Shore, Burt's acknowledged "best friend," who sang a moving rendition of AMERICA THE BEAUTIFUL, bringing a tear to Burt's eye. Later, Dinah would tell the audience that Burt "had done more for little old ladies in tennis shoes than any one else in the world."

If Burt graciously accepted the awards and the publicity, he preferred keeping a low public profile over his fury concerning the continuing, unsolved murders of black children in Atlanta. When all the TV and movie stars decided to hold a "telethon" to raise money in order to keep the Atlanta Police Force amply funded, Burt agreed to participate on the condition that no mention be made of SHARKY'S MACHINE, which was in production in Atlanta at the time In no way did he want to personally capitalize on the tragedy. Privately and without fanfare, he donated $10,000 of his own money to the cause.

As 1981 came to a close, Burt was back on the TV trail, plugging SHARKY'S MACHINE into one of the "big" pictures of the Christmas season. SHARKY'S MACHINE grossed nearly $30 million its first two months in release, topped only by TAPS and NEIGHBORS in holiday season box-office. SHARKY'S MACHINE did far better in the larger, urban communities than it did down south, where Burt's movies traditionally made their money. Coming on the heels of his Friar's Roast, and his Hollywood Boulevard star, it's not hard to see why the South might reject *Sharky* in favor of *Smokey*. The question was, could Burt?

It was on one of those local, A.M. talk shows, "Good Morning L.A.," while promoting SHARKY while Burt met the woman many feel

might finally make it as the next Mrs. Burt
Reynolds. For the first time in nearly ten years
Burt was living completely alone. Just this past
summer he had been best man at Hal Needham's
wedding. Needham had decided to try marriage
again. The woman he chose to make Mrs. Needham was Burt's one-time fellow Universal contract player's widow, Mrs. David Janssen.

He arrived at the ABC-TV studios a few
minutes before air-time, 9:00 A.M. It was then
than Burt first laid eyes on Tawny Little, Miss
America 1976, co-host of the popular L.A. talk
show. Born Tawny Godin, she was married for a
brief time after her one-year reign as Miss
America. Keeping her married name, she moved
from New York to Los Angeles, eventually landing a job in television. Tall, demure, part-Indian
with coal-black eyes and dazzling white teeth,
Tawny mused prettily as Burt gushed and
swarmed, the familiar Reynolds grin lit once
more by the snap of a beautiful woman's glaze.
Tawny Little was, in many ways, like
SHARKY'S MACHINE—a revelation, a revital-
ization, a triumph. The lingering question was
the same; could Burt embrace the new while re-
taining past.

The last American hero. Into the eighties with
a quarter-century of action, adventure, and romance behind him, and a wide-open future
ahead. Tawny Little, the latest in a long line of
Reynolds hopefuls might indeed make it to the
altar, but regardless of how things turned out,
she'd already accompanied Burt to the tree

house, spending Christmas with him down on the ranch, meeting the folks. And, she was there in L.A. when Burt's friends celebrated his quarter-century in show business, an affair televised on network TV early in 1982, gaining top ratings. Burt's TV appeal was so strong that during those months when ratings were used to set advertising revenues for the coming year, Burt himself, or one of his movies, could be found almost any given night on one of the networks. The "celebration" was broadcast in such a month, placing number two for its week in the ratings book, causing a celebration at the network of another kind.

Rumors flew out of L.A. that Burt had given Tawny a diamond engagement ring, that they were secretly planning a June wedding, that Burt was settling down with one woman at last. However, before the smear was dry on that rumor's ink, the word came down that Tawny and Burt were through, that Burt had found yet another special lady, Loni Anderson, and as far as Tawny was concerned, all bets were off.

While the world speculated about his latest flame, Burt was setting the Burt Reynolds Theatre on fire directing a volatile production of ONE FLEW OVER THE CUCKOO'S NEST, starring his pal, Martin Sheen, in the role Nicholson had done in the movies, the role Burt would have done anything to play. And, to top it all, a poll taken among the country's teenagers showed Burt as their number one favorite American "Hero," coming in ahead of Ronald Reagan.

At the age of forty-six, he could look back on

his life with pride. The little mullet with the chip on his shoulder had finally been accepted. He'd never stopped running, from the football field to the top of the film industry, limited only by what his imagination could conjure. He was in love with the love America had for him, and he was at last beginning to be able to live with that love, not afraid to embrace his own image. He'd met the challenges along the way, struggling when it seemed he'd never make it, pushing himself when no one else could understand why, still leaning against the wind.

Finally, the last image is Burt alone, in close-up, on the wide-screen of everyone's imagination. The face, with the ever-loving smile belongs to the gentleman in jeans; every guy's older brother, every woman's dream lover.

OTHER BOOKS BY MARC ELIOT:

Death Of A Rebel:
Starring Phil Ochs and a Small Circle of Friends

American Television:
The Official Art of the Artificial

Marc Eliot was born and raised in New York City. He currei tly divides his time between New York, Hollywood, and Palenville.

The author on Sunset Boulevard.
(Photo by A.G.)